Brain Science

About Narcoleptic, Degenerative and Other Diseases

By Sally Stephens

Table of Contents

The History

The very first convincing descriptions of narcolepsy-cataplexy were reported in Germany by Westphal (1877) and Fisher (1878). The distinct association of episodes of muscle weakness set off by enjoyment and drowsiness were defined in these 2 reports. In both cases, genetic aspects were kept in mind, with the mom of Westphal's client and one sister of Fisher's client providing narcolepsy signs. The leading hypothesis to clarify narcolepsy at the time was to describe the well advertised case of von Zastrow. Von Zastrow was a just recently apprehended pathological rapist extensively really believed to experience pathological drowsiness as a result of quelched homosexuality and extreme masturbation.

Gélineau (1880) is commonly acknowledged for giving narcolepsy its name and for acknowledging the condition as a particular scientific entity. Its description of a red wine cask maker with narcolepsy in la Gazette des hôpitaux de Paris was classical but Gélineau did not strictly distinguish muscle weakness episodes and sleep attacks set off by feelings. Rather, Gelineau suggested a typical physiology for these 2 signs. Loëwenfeld (1902), was the very first to give a name to muscle weakness episodes activated by feelings or cataplexy.

The 1917-1927 epidemic of sleeping sickness lethargica resulted in a restored interest in narcolepsy and sleep research but also added much confusion to the nosological meaning of narcolepsy. Sleeping sickness lethargica typically presented at first with somnolence and the term narcolepsy was usually used to define any form of daytime drowsiness. The association of somnolence and occulomotor paralysis also caused the leader work of Von Economo (1930) and the acknowledgment of the posterior hypothalamus as a vital area for the big promotion of wakefulness In simple fact, Von Economo should be credited as being among the very first private investigators to properly propose that an area in the posterior hypothalamus was lesioned in human narcolepsy. In 1930, he wrote: it is extremely likely, though not shown, that the narcolepsy of Gelineau, Westphal and Redlich has its main cause in an yet unidentified illness of that area.

As narcolepsy with cataplexy was also observed sometimes of sleeping sickness lethargica, clinicians long disputed the presence of idiopathic narcolepsy and the value of cataplexy for specifying the scientific entity. Big case series of narcolepsy-cataplexy were reported by Addie (1926) Wilson (1927and Daniels (1934). The evaluation by Daniels is thought about by a lot of as one of the most informative medical evaluations released to this date. More work at the Mayo Center, by Yoss and Daly) and in Prague by Bedrich Roth, then caused the timeless description of the narcolepsy tetrad.

Different techniques were at first proposed in the treatment of narcolepsy, consisting of intrathecal injection of air, cerebrospinal fluid elimination and X-ray irradiation of the hypothalamic area. Ephedrine treatment was normally used as the only partially reliable treatment for daytime drowsiness till Prinzmetal and Bloomberg introduced amphetamines in 1935. Yoss and Daly introduced methylphenidate in the 1960s. Quickly after the discovery of tricyclic antidepressants in 1957, Akimoto, Honda and Takahashi used imipramine in the treatment of human cataplexy, developing the double stimulant/antidepressant medicinal treatment most typically used in narcoleptic clients to this date.

Rapid Eye Movement

The early descriptions of Rapid Eye Movement and its associated atonia led several private investigators to study sleep start in narcolepsy Vogel (1960) was the very first to report Rapid Eye Movement sleep at sleep start in a narcoleptic client, an observation extended by Rechschaffen and Dement several years later. Together with Hishikawa who studied the EEG of narcoleptic subjects throughout sleep paralysis and hypnagogic hallucinations, these authors articulated the now classical hypothesis of dissociated Rapid Eye Movement to clarify some of the signs of narcolepsy. This discovery also caused the facility of the several sleep latency tests as a basic diagnostic test for narcolepsy.

In spite of the development, the early postwar duration was stuffed with psychoanalytical descriptions for narcolepsy-cataplexy. Together with Kleitman, who actually believed narcolepsy was a natural condition including unusual carotid stimulation reflexes Daniels, was amongst the couple of to actually believe in the natural nature of narcolepsy. In a letter to Kleitman dated July 21, 1948, Daniels wrote: I was especially thinking about your views concerning the importance of narcolepsy, since I came to the exact same conclusion early in the course of my research studies and have been distinctly irritated by current efforts of the psychosomaticists to restore the old idea that narcolepsy is just a type of escape.

Meaning

Narcolepsy is categorized as a persistent sleep condition and is thought about a persistent neural condition that is brought on by the failure of a person's brain to manage sleep-wake cycles correctly. A private suffering with narcolepsy experiences daytime drowsiness and unmanageable bouts of going to sleep throughout the day. People experiencing narcolepsy are not able to stay awake for extended periods of time and victims drop off to sleep at an unsuitable spot or time often without caution.

Other far more serious signs experienced by a specific with narcolepsy consist of a condition called cataplexy which is an unexpected loss of muscle tone that can trigger physical changes like slurred speech or muscle weakness. Cataplexy is typically set off by extreme feelings and is unmanageable.

Another condition that might happen for people struggling with narcolepsy is sleep paralysis where the individual temporarily is not able to speak or move while going to sleep or waking. People with narcolepsy also struggle with hypnagogic hallucinations which are dream-like auditory or visual hallucination experienced with a person is dozing or going to sleep.

A common sleep-wake cycle for an individual without narcolepsy is early phase of sleep, much deeper phase of sleep, and after that after around 90 minutes Rapid Eye Movement (rapid-eye-movement sleep) sleep. For a private struggling with narcolepsy the Rapid Eye Movement phase takes place nearly instantly after they drop off to sleep in addition to regularly throughout their waking hours.

This illness can impact a specific at any age, but normally happens between the ages of 15 and 25. It is also more typical in guys than ladies. It is a really under identified disease, usually believed to be anxiety, epilepsy, or a negative effects of medication. Tons of people struggling with narcolepsy are never ever appropriately detected though the illness is really disabling to their life. It can hinder a person's work, social life, individual relationships, and make them more susceptible to mishaps.

The reason for this illness is not understood; nevertheless, it is actually believed that genes play an important aspect. A little percent of people experiencing this sleeping condition have a close relative that also struggles with the illness.

A person ought to look for medical guidance if they experience extreme drowsiness throughout the daytime - extreme to the point where it disrupts their individual and/or expert life. The medical physician will likely refer the individual to a sleep professional who will identify the primary problem and decide on its seriousness. Medical diagnoses can include an evaluation of the person's sleep history; a polysomnogram (test that gauges sleep signals through electrodes on the scalp); and a numerous sleep latency test (test which gauge just how long it takes a private to go to sleep throughout the day). Both the polysomnogram and several sleep latency tests are carried out in a medical center or a sleep center.

There is also no treatment for this sleeping condition but there is treatment. Treatment depends upon the real seriousness of the person's narcolepsy which is determined by screening. Treatment is customized to the individual and can include way of life changes like the guideline of sleep schedule, scheduling of daytime naps, keeping away from caffeine or alcohol, developing a workout regimen, and a meal schedule to help in reducing the signs. A medical professional might also try drug treatment by recommending a stimulant drug to help keep the individual struggling with narcolepsy awake throughout the day, or an antidepressant drug that reduces the Rapid Eye Movement cycle.

Some Realities about Narcolepsy

The main sign of narcolepsy is an overstated and nearly frustrating drowsiness throughout the daytime, even after a good night's sleep. Another sign is sleep that is typically disrupted by regularly getting up.

In the most serious cases, people struggling with this sleeping condition will go to sleep involuntarily sometimes and spots that are unsuitable and can be unsafe too. These "sleep attacks" last from just several seconds to more than half an hour. They happen with no cautions whatsoever and make keeping a typical work schedule or individual relationship really tough, if not unrealistic.

Narcoleptics do not have the vibrant separation between wakefulness and sleep that the majority of us have. A lot of patients have reported that the difference between being awake and being sleeping is usually tough to figure out. This might be because of the simple fact that narcoleptics most often drop off to sleep straight into the dream wealthy Rapid Eye Movement state without slowly advancing through the non-REM phases first.

In addition to daytime drowsiness there are other signs too but these might, or might not, exist in all cases.

Cataplexy. This is an unexpected muscle weakness really comparable to the extremity paralysis that takes place naturally throughout Rapid Eye Movement. It will last from just several seconds to some minutes and takes place while the person is awake. Cataplexy appears to be activated by a fast psychological response of some sort like laughter, anger, worry, or surprise. This abrupt muscle weakness can trigger anything from drooping facial muscles to a total collapse. Sleep Paralysis. This is a short-term failure to speak or move when suffering a narcoleptic episode. People with this sign find themselves unable to move or talk both when dropping off to sleep and when awakening.

Hypnologic Dreams. These are exceptionally brilliant dreams that happen when narcoleptics very first drop off to sleep. Hypnologic dreams are so reasonable they regularly are puzzled with reality.

Sleep scientists approximate that approximately 350,000 Americans experience narcolepsy but less than 50,000 have been properly identified. If this evaluation is precise, these numbers would make narcolepsy more prevalent than Parkinson's illness or Several Sclerosis.

Narcolepsy is extremely hard to identify and specifically in those who have only the daytime drowsiness sign. It is most regularly misinterpreted for anxiety or epilepsy, or perhaps the adverse effects of other medications.

Right medical diagnosis is frequently determined through making use of a polysomnogram over night sleep taping test (PSG) and a Numerous Sleep Latency Test (MSLT). Both of these tests will show the indications of going to sleep rapidly and straight into Rapid Eye Movement.

While narcolepsy can take place at any time, the signs most regularly appear while still in teenage years or extremely early the adult years. Genes appear to play a part in addition to one in 10 narcoleptics have a close member of the family who is also narcoleptic.

Current research has exposed that narcoleptics do not appear to have a neurotransmitter called hypocretin whose job it is to make sure wakefulness. The existing theory is that maybe an autoimmune response triggered by illness, genetics, or brain injury, damages the cells that produce hypocretin but more research is needed.
One Of The Most Typical Signs

Narcolepsy is a persistent condition triggered by a decrease in a protein in the brain called orexin. There is strong proof to suggest that narcolepsy is actually an auto-immune illness.

Signs of Narcolepsy
1. Extreme Daytime Drowsiness (EDS).
At its core this is what narcolepsy is - being tired all the time. EDS will continue even if a complete nights rest is had.

2. Cataplexy.
Cataplexy is loss of motor muscle control. You might experience abrupt loss of motor control even while awake. This can be caused with high feelings like sobbing.

3. Sleep Paralysis.
Sleep paralysis is a sign where you are not able to physically move at the start and/or end of your sleep.

4. Automatic Conduct.
This is where you continue to work when you are asleep, and when you awaken you have no memory of the event.

5. Microsleeps.
A microsleep is when you go to sleep for a brief time without caution and generally not remembering you where actually asleep.

6. Hypnagogic hallucinations.
These hallucinations are vibrant, dream experiences and can happen anytime you are sleeping, dozing off, microsleeping and so on.

7. Quick entry into Rapid-eye-movement sleep (Rapid Eye Movement) sleep.
Narcoleptics are distinct in that they can go into Rapid Eye Movement at the start of their sleep, without needing to wait the typical 90 minutes a regular person would require to get in Rapid Eye Movement.

8. Evening Wakefulness.

It's practically an oxymoron that Narcoleptics, who are going to sleep all the time, would have an issue with wakefulness. But sometimes you might have severe durations of awareness at odd hours in the night.

9. Irregular Brainwave Rhythms.
Generally when you are awake your brainwaves show a routine rhythm, though narcoleptics typically have irregular brainwaves because of getting in and leaving sleep cycles spontaneously.

Some Typical Causes

People with Narcolepsy condition always tend to have trouble to stay awake. They can drop off to sleep really all of a sudden throughout the day. It is just like a sleep attacks to them. Even after they had adequate sleep, they can still quickly drop off to sleep. This uncommon sleeping issue is actually impacting their social life, work and daily life.

There are 2 type of sleep that is non rapid-eye-movement sleep and rapid-eye-movement sleep. For typical people, they will go through the non-rapid eye movement sleep initially right before rapid-eye-movement sleep duration. But it's different for people with narcolepsy. They generally will go through the rapid-eye-movement sleep initially right before the non rapid-eye-movement sleep.

Just because of the, they generally will lose their muscle tone when they get up. Worst, this muscle tone and loose of control can make them collapse. They also will be getting sleep paralysis that means they will not have the ability to speak and even move no matter while they were getting up or being up to sleep. And when they get up, they also tend to see hallucinations.

According to some research, it was specified that the primary reason for narcolepsy is the brain which are absence of hypocretin chemical that works to promotes the cells in the brain to give wakefulness. The reason for the absence of the hypocretin chemical in people with narcolepsy is still unidentified. Nevertheless, there are some aspects that were understood to be the reasons for the absence of hypocretin, which is tension, and brain injury. If there's a brain injury, there will be some loss of certain brain cells. Other elements are infection, and also changes of hormonal agents. Nonetheless, it was also found that couple of varieties of people with narcolepsy has associated with their loved ones also with narcolepsy. Meaning, some people acquired the propensity of having narcolepsy condition from their loved ones.

Concerning the inheritance of narcolepsy, research has been made and it was been recognized that gene also triggers narcolepsy. Hypothalamus belongs to the brain that promotes sleep conduct and the gene will paves the way to the cells in hypothalamus to get messages from other cells in the brain. Nevertheless, of the gene is not typical, those cells will not have the ability to link and communicate usually and this is why the irregular of the sleeping patterns happen.

It does run in the family for some people, but the majority of them with narcolepsy, they do not connect to any of their relative that suffers the exact same condition. In conclusion, it does not mean that if you do not have any loved ones with narcolepsy, you will not get it.

Medical diagnosis Requirements

If you feel exceedingly worn out throughout the day, you can use the narcolepsy medical diagnosis requirements to discover if narcolepsy is very likely to be the reason for your issues. Let me clarify how the requirements work, and how comprehending the nature of cataplexy can help you find suitable treatment.

Narcolepsy is a seriously under-diagnosed illness - it's believed to impact over 200,000 people in the United States, but only a quarter of those are detected. This is mainly as the intensity of narcolepsy differs so much.

While it's instantly apparent in some patients, other ones generally experience drowsiness with periodic additional signs, which can be tough to favorably identify. By comprehending narcolepsy medical diagnosis requirements, you and your doctor can choose whether you're very likely to be struggling with this condition.

Within the International category of sleep conditions (ICSD) handbook there are 2 sets of very little requirements for detecting narcolepsy. Among them in narcolepsy when the patient has cataplexy

Narcolepsy Medical Diagnosis Criteria When the Victim Has Cataplexy
The very first set of requirements is used for identifying narcolepsy is if you struggle with cataplexy.

Cataplexy is an abrupt, unforeseen loss of muscle function. This can trigger a total collapse of the body, but may also be less serious and just include a short-term sagging of facial functions, weakness at the neck or knees, or slurred speech.

If you experience cataplexy along with lapsing into sleep throughout the day most days, that suffices to identify narcolepsy. But not all cases of narcolepsy consist of cataplexy, in which case extra signs really need to be observed in addition to drowsiness to make a medical diagnosis.

If You Experience Narcolepsy and Cataplexy
Being detected with narcolepsy and cataplexy is a typical way to be detected with narcolepsy. Fortunately is there work treatments for this condition.

Formerly, dexamphetamine was used for all narcolepsy treatments. Although it had substantial downsides in the form of negative effects and dependence, for a long period of time it was the only treatment readily available.

Now there is a brand-new, more remarkable treatment readily available in the form of modavigil. Modavigil (modafinil) is a brand-new and reliable treatment for narcolepsy clients, even if they have cataplexy too.

Modavigil has practically no negative effects, is inexpensive, efficient, and simple to get. See your doctor concerning modavigil as a possible treatment for you or your really loved one with narcolepsy and cataplexy.

Value of Seeing the Manifestations

For many individuals, the battle to stay awake when they really need to is a day-to-day fight. Narcolepsy impacts about one in 2,000 people worldwide and it begins relatively early in life for those who have a hereditary predisposition to the condition. Since people differ significantly in brain makeup and vulnerability to ecological triggers, narcolepsy signs might differ significantly in intensity between those who struggle with this condition.

For many people, narcolepsy signs start to appear between the ages of 10 and 25. Once the condition develops, it doesn't disappear, even with treatment. Whether you are cooking, working, driving, and even taking pleasure in an adventure trip, you can drop off to sleep. Nevertheless, changes in way of life and brand-new insights into medical treatments can help in reducing the signs to enable you to live a complete and active life.

There are 2 main signs. The very first is "extreme daytime drowsiness" and the other is "unusual Rapid Eye Movement". This can lead to sleep paralysis when you are not able to move or speak upon going to sleep or waking, hallucinations which can be visual or acoustic and can in some cases be frightening, and particularly cataplexy. This latter sign is an unexpected loss of muscle control usually found with severe feelings and is special to the condition of narcolepsy.

Usually this condition is tough to detect because many individuals suffer severe fatigue throughout the day, but flop to understand some of the other indications that signal they struggle with this condition. Physician, for that reason, should search for other signs which tons of do not even know they have.

Among the most special functions of the condition is what medical experts call "microsleep". These are extremely short bouts of sleep where an individual continues to operate as though they're awake. They continue to talk, walk around, and put things away, but then have no memory of what they just did. In addition, they typically wake regularly during the night when they experience an increased heart rate, hot flashes, and are often so alert they cannot return to sleep.

When they do drop off to sleep they go into Rapid Eye Movement rather quickly. For many people this takes about 90 minutes. People with this condition will also have really brilliant dreams or feel paralyzed at the start of their sleep cycle even if it happens throughout the day. If you feel you might experience narcolepsy signs, it is very important to look for a medical examination instantly, as continuing to operate while sleeping and having actually an interrupted sleep cycle can be incredibly unsafe.

Basically, those with this condition will wind up dropping off to sleep without any way to manage it. This condition is usually the outcome of a hereditary condition, and there is no recognized remedy for the condition since yet. Nevertheless, you can take control of the condition by following some of the pointers beneath to help manage your sleeping patterns and conquer the condition.

Make the effort and speak with your doctor about all of the different choices readily available for therapy. Talking to somebody who has a specialized in sleep conditions will help you to take control of your life and organize it. It will help you to stay away from any narcoleptic fits and also help you on a psychological level to conquer this condition that is attempting to manage your life.

Speak with your medical professional and inquire about medications for your condition. Stimulants work by keeping a ton of clients up throughout the daytime, but when it comes time to go to bed in the evening they are unable to since the medication has not worn away. Antidepressants help to remove your Rapid Eye Movement cycle. People who are experiencing narcolepsy can help stop sensation tired throughout the day by utilizing salt oxybate.

Ensure that you are arranging routine times for sleep. Getting sleep on a constant basis can help stop narcolepsy. It is oftentimes the insane sleep patterns that wind up causing narcolepsy in the very first spot. If you have the ability to go to sleep at the exact same time regularly and get up at the exact same time every early morning, you will have the ability to require your body into preserving a correct sleep schedule. No matter whether it is throughout the week or the weekend, you really need to keep the exact same patterns throughout the period to help manage your sleep schedule.

Do not forget working out. Workout has been shown very helpful to a ton of people who are experiencing narcolepsy. When you work out it helps to put your body into a state of natural sleep and manage your system. Just like you can make the effort to follow a particular sleep schedule, you can make the effort to make certain that you are working out every day to get rid of feeling the results of narcolepsy.

Drink drinks that are very good for you. Prevent anything which contains alcohol, caffeine or nicotine. These 3 compounds trigger the body's natural cycle to get knocked for a loop, which can result in some of the most unpredictable sleeping patterns out there. When you keep away from the triggers, together with developing a constant sleep and workout regimen will help your body to stay away from falling under the phases of narcolepsy.

Simply because you have been detected with narcolepsy doesn't mean that you need to let it manage your life. You have the power to be able to take control of the condition by following several easy pointers and tricks to help you live an efficient and interesting way of life. Take control of your condition at last with the correct changes in your life and health. In the end, you will find a ton of advantages with having the ability to go throughout the day without the worry of dropping off to sleep right where you are.

You can live a regular life devoid of narcolepsy if you only make the effort to learn the appropriate upkeep strategies and make them part of your regimen. Do not let the condition control you, but instead it is time that you take control into your own hands.

Narcolepsy in Kids

Kids who struggle with narcolepsy often find it challenging to go to sleep. They feel exhausted throughout the day, but still find it challenging to sleep. Narcoleptic attacks can take place at any time. The level of drowsiness is putting your kid at danger. No matter what activity your kid is carrying out, it might experience a narcoleptic attack.

Another fascinating simple fact is that kids with narcolepsy do not have light sleep; they fall straight to deep sleep. The deep sleep stage in which the straight go to is Rapid Eye Movement (Rapid-eye-movement sleep). Kids with narcolepsy can go to deep sleep at any time when they are awake. In some circumstances this can be extremely damaging for kids with narcolepsy.

Kids with this sort of sleeping condition find it hard-to-impossible to stay awake at random moment throughout the day. Narcolepsy in kids isn't an absence of sleep; they may be sleeping the entire night and still be tired the next day. This is what we know as EDS (Excessive Day Sleep). Extreme Day Sleep is one sign or narcolepsy in kids. When somebody goes to sleep, they lose control over the majority of the body's muscles as they are resting. There is a condition in which this happens when they head out of sleep - cataplexy. Cataplexy resembles sleep paralysis and happens into Rapid Eye Movement.

Some kids are experiencing hallucinations when they are getting up from a sleep - hypnopompic hallucinations. Hpnagogic hallucination is the exact same but when dropping off to sleep. These hallucinations can consist of some other senses too. Extreme Day Sleep, cataplexy, sleep paralysis and hallucinations are all signs of narcolepsy in kids. Narcolepsy in kids is not a night horror.

Correct sleep is greatly crucial for growing kids. Without the correct dosage of a great night's sleep, your kid can experience numerous cognitive concerns that can affect his scholastic undertakings. A lot of sleep conditions can quickly be managed with the aid of correct diet plan and way of life changes. Nevertheless, a lot of other sleep disorders can become a headache for a life time if you aren't cautious in the starting years. Thankfully, Narcolepsy can be managed.

What is Narcolepsy?
Narcolepsy is a sleep condition that is defined by extreme drowsiness that affects the daily life of a patient. The significant signs of Narcolepsy consist of:

Consistent drowsiness in the day hours
Failure to preserve wakefulness
Hypnagogic hallucinations
Sleep paralysis
Cataplexy
Unexpectedly going to sleep throughout uncommon hours and having no control over the sleep pattern

How do I know my kid has it?
Narcolepsy is rather simple to discover. If your kid goes to sleep on the breakfast table or stops working to preserve wakefulness while messing around a school play area devices in school, instantly contact your healthcare professional. Ask your kid about his condition and see if he experiences any of the above discussed signs.

Workout and Narcolepsy
There is no particular medication or treatment that will totally remove the indications of Narcolepsy. A growing body of research shows that a kid who is highly active with routine activity in outside play area devices, or any play ground for that matter, hardly ever develops Narcolepsy. Your kid's healthcare expert may recommend certain medications in addition to way of life changes. The most typical medications for Narcolepsy consist of dextroamphetamine (Dexedrine), methylphenidate (Ritalin) and dextroamphetamine (Adderal), among other ones.

What can you do?
Sleep conditions are normally a result of inappropriate diet plan and sleep. Kids, in contrast to grownups need correct sleep to preserve their health, and absence of sufficient sleep or irregular sleep patterns can hinder their physical and cognitive development. Here is a well-sorted list of things that you can do to stop Narcolepsy in your kid:

Preserve a routine sleep pattern of around 14 hours for young children and 10-12 hours for young children.
Stay away from letting your kids feast on processed food. Prepare a balance diet plan and help your kids grow with healthy foods and vitamins.
Change made fruit juices with homemade fruit juices. Engage your kids with healthy exercise. Whether it's church play area devices or a backyard sand pit, any backyard can help kids increase their chances of a healthy living. So, let your kid out in the play area.
How to Manage Narcolepsy

Narcolepsy is just among the sleep conditions that people can suffer through. It is specified as the start of a desire to go to sleep that the person cannot manage. This condition can cause the victim going to sleep in a scenario that can be incredibly harmful and unsuitable. Can you envision what it would be kind of like if you were to drop off to sleep behind the wheel of an automobile? Think of all of the people you would be jeopardizing if that were to happen. Luckily, there are several different approaches that you can use to help handle the condition regularly.

Put in the time to set up a nap in throughout the day. Something as easy as a fifteen or half an hour nap after your lunch break and night meal will help lessen the chance that you will go to sleep all of a sudden throughout the day. Arrange the time in to stop any prospective episodes when you least expect it.

Have a bit of caffeine. Not everybody who has narcolepsy will take advantage of caffeine, but there are a ton of times where the patient can find solace in a cup of coffee or tea. It will help to promote your body and stop you from going to sleep throughout the day.

Think about using an antidepressant. Some narcoleptics will have the ability to gain from SSRIs. They help to offer you with a sense of balance that helps restrict the chance of being overwhelmed with the desire to go to sleep.

Ask your medical professional about using a sleep help. Among the largest things for somebody who is experiencing narcolepsy is that they might experience the desire to sleep throughout the day. Nevertheless, when it comes time to go to bed during the night they wind up experiencing not being able sleep. As a result, they are unable to sleep when they really need it the most and just because of the they are a lot more worn out throughout the daytime. If this holds true with your particular circumstances, you might really want a prescription sleep help to help you get the rest you really need at night. This will enable you to get a complete night of rest and get up sensation revitalized and all set to take on the day. You will not be as susceptible to dropping off to sleep throughout the day since you will be getting the rest that you really need throughout the night.

Stay away from any foods that could trigger sleepiness throughout the day. Foods that are high in starches and carbs can help to bring your body down and make you sleepy. When your body goes through the abrupt burst in sugar, it will help the narcolepsy kick into equipment and the sleep will come on without caution. As you restrict your consumption of these sugar enriched foods, you will be assisting to keep your body well balanced and devoid of the chemicals that make you want to sleep.

Attempt to organize your schedule to decrease the effect of narcolepsy starting. If you are somebody who handles break outs in the afternoon, you should try scheduling a conference or an errand throughout the early morning to stop any disturbances or invasions with your sleep patterns. Attempt to travel with a good friend as much as you perhaps can. That way if you do tend to drop off to sleep it will not put anybody at danger or at risk. The essence is to try to look after anything essential when you are most likely to stay awake. Otherwise, you will never ever have the ability to get anything done and it will be a perpetual cycle to attempting to remain on top of the condition.

Narcolepsy can be managed once you discover what you are doing to help manage the condition. There is no reason you should feel as though you are stuck sleeping all the time since there is plenty that can be done to get rid of the condition and take control of your life. Take

pleasure in all of the flexibility you can have with narcolepsy when you discover what you can do to conquer the condition.
Ayurvedic Treatment with Herbs

Narcolepsy is a persistent sleep condition defined by frustrating day-time sleepiness and unexpected attacks of sleep, which might trigger serious interruptions in life. Typical symptoms and signs consist of extreme day-time drowsiness, unexpected loss of muscle tone, sleep paralysis, hallucinations, automated conduct and agitated, night-time sleep. Genes and a disrupted resistance are the recognized causes for this condition.

The Ayurvedic treatment of narcolepsy is targeted at increasing night-time sleep and decreasing day-time bouts of drowsiness. A mix of sedatives and stimulants are used for this purpose. Medicines like Brahmi-Vati, Saraswatarishta, Laxmi-Vilas-Ras, Maha-Laxmi-Vilas-Ras, Dashmoolarishta, Arjunarishta, Maha-Vat-Vidhwans-Ras, Makar-Dhwaj Ras, Abhrak-Bhasma, Suvarna-Bhasma and Bruhat-Vat-Chintamani are used for this purpose. Organic medications which can be used in this condition are: Brahmi (Bacopa monnieri), Jatamansi (Nardostachys jatamansi), Sarpagandha (Rauwolfia serpentina), Mandukparni (Centella asiatica), Shankhpushpi (Convolvulus pluricaulis), Vacha (Acorus calamus), Guduchi (Tinospora cordifolia), Tagar (Valeriana wallichii), Nirgundi (Vitex negundo), Vishwa (Zinziber officinalis), Marich (Piper nigrum), Pippali (Piper longum), Chitrak (Plumbago zeylanica), Chavya (Piper retrofractrum), Kuchla (Strychnos nuxvomica), Ashwagandha (Withania somnifera), Rasna (Pluchea lanceolata), Erandmool (Ricinus communis), Shalparni (Desmodium gangeticum) and Prushnaparni (Uraria picta). It is necessary to keep in mind that treatment needs to be custom-made for each individual client and adjustments made in treatment, after getting feedback from the client.

Some Panchkarma treatments can be put to great usage in the treatment of narcolepsy. In the process called 'Snehan', the whole body is rubbed with medicated oils like Mahanarayan oil, Mahamash oil, Chandan- Bala-Laxadi oil and oil of Sesame. This is followed by 'Swedan' in which steam fomentation is offered to the whole body using medications like Dashmool-Qadha and Nirgundi-Qadha. 'Nasya' treatment can be done in this condition, which includes instilling nasal drops like Vacha oil, Marich oil, and liquid extracts of Shigru (Moringa oleifera) and Vishwa (Zinziber officinalis). Medicated enemas can also be given using medications like Vishgarbha oil. The restorative purpose of all the above discussed Panchkarma treatments is to decrease the 'Kapha' dosha and control the 'Barrel' dosha; this in turn decreases extreme day-time sleepiness and sleep attacks.

With appropriate medications and the suitable way of life adjustments, many clients of narcolepsy can appropriately adjust to their condition. People impacted by this condition must stay away from long drives, nicotine and alcohol. They should work out routinely, follow a repaired day-time schedule, take regular naps, and take into self-confidence their good friends and associates concerning their condition.

Treatment for Narcolepsy
As far as treatment for narcolepsy goes, medication and changes to one's way of life can manage the signs of the condition. Narcolepsy nevertheless cannot by treated totally using medication. The more unwanted signs of the condition that include Cataplexy and EDS can be jailed.

Stimulants
In order to help people with narcolepsy stay awake and alert throughout the day, stimulants like Modafinil (Provigil) or methylphenidate (Ritalin) are used. The previous is a reasonably brand-new medication used as a treatment for narcolepsy signs and is also less addicting than older stimulants. The latter has been around for a longer duration and like other older stimulants, can in some cases produce negative effects like palpitation and anxiety.

Modafinil as a Treatment for Narcolepsy
Presently modafinil is the remarkable narcolepsy treatment for lots of reasons:

- It's non-addictive

- It does not develop ecstasy or a 'high'.

- It has a long half life of 12-15 hours (this means you just need to take one dosage in the early morning).

- It does not 'burn the brain out' and users can cease and feel regular instantly.

- It's low-cost as lower dosages are needed less typically.

- There is no chance for abuse potential (unlike dexamphetamine which has a huge abuse potential).

So as you can see, it's light-years ahead of any other narcoleptic treatment.

Antidepressants.
Antidepressants are used as a treatment for narcolepsy signs like cataplexy or sleep paralysis, which are connected with Rapid Eye Movement. These medications intend to reduce Rapid Eye Movement and therefore minimize the signs connected with it. They also help stop hypnagogic hallucinations that people experiencing narcolepsy may have. Antidepressants administered for this condition consist of Imipramine (Tofranil) and Protriptyline (Vivactil). Fluoxetine (Prozac, Sarafem) and Sertraline (Zoloft) which are Serotonin reuptake inhibitors (SSRIs) are also used as antidepressants.

Salt oxybate (Xyrem) is also another drug that helps in managing Cataplexy. It also helps people experiencing narcolepsy get much better sleep throughout the night. When the dose is increased, it also minimizes sleepiness throughout the daytime. The drug nevertheless is understood to produce negative effects like bed-wetting, sleepwalking and shortness of breath, which has triggered the FDA to manage the drug extremely strictly.

Way of life modifications are also a natural and efficient form of treatment for narcolepsy. People can keep away from heavy meals, alcohol or caffeine right before going to sleep. They also really need to follow a rigorous bedtime schedule. They can have brief 10 to 15 minute naps throughout the day to manage drowsiness. Preserving a healthy diet plan, having great workout for the body and living a healthy way of life would considerably minimize the signs of narcolepsy.

Diet plans for Narcolepsy.

Stay away from:
. Avoid alcohol and sugar
. Stay away from stimulants like coffee, caffeinated beverages, tea or drugs.

Do:
. Make a schedule and keep time of sleep
. Stay away from shift work or preserve timing of the shift
. Take brief naps throughout the day
. Set up naps, like 15 minute nap after lunch then 15 minutes nap at 5:30 pm. This will supply short-lived awareness and lower the strength of daytime drowsiness.

Take in:
. Minimize consumption of fats
. Boost consumption of omega-3 fats, it secures the cell membranes and the myeline sheath of the nerves
. Boost consumption of fibers
. Boost consumption of calcium and magnesium, needed for energy production and correct performance of nerve system
. Take in food high in protein diet plan throughout the day, protein foods increases awareness
. Take in foods which contain all vital amino acids
. Food high in proteins consists of L - Glutamine (amino acid), it promotes brainpower and is a brain fuel as it passes the brain barrier easily
. You can take L - Glutamine supplements, empty stomach with water or juice. Do not drink milk with it, as it impedes the absorption. You can have vitamin C and vitamin B6 supplements together with it for better absorption
. Take in proteins high in L - Tyrosine; it is needed for production of norepinephrine and dopamine which are necessary for psychological awareness and long term memory
. Take in food high in L - tryptophan at night meals with carbs as they slow psychological function and trigger drowsiness.
- Milk, tuna fish, turkey and eggs, Almonds, cabbage, kidney beans, oats, pistachios, bananas, poppy seeds, pumpkin seeds, spinach, wheat, sunflower seeds and night primrose seeds

. Take in complex carbs for night meals as they have relaxing impact and might back drowsiness. Although carb soothes brain but is needed for appropriate psychological efficiency as glucose is primary fuel source for brain
. Take in food high in choline or lecithin. Choline serves as a neurotransmitter and is extremely crucial for brain function.
- Milk, eggs, liver, wheat bacterium and peanuts are wealthy in choline.
- Other sources are beef, shrimp, salmon, Atlantic cod, Brussels sprouts, broccoli and milk chocolate
. Take in food high in chromium; it promotes energy and manages sugar metabolic process
. Take in coenzyme Q10, it increases blood circulation to the brain
. Food sources:
- Meat poultry, fish, soybean, canola oil and nuts, fruits veggies, eggs, dairy items are also great sources
. You can take supplements of coenzyme Q10 - 100-300 mg each day
. Take in Octocosanol supplements. It is a naturally happening compound found in sugar walking cane, wheat bacterium oil, spinach and other health food sources. It increases the oxygen usage by the body
. Take in B vitamins particularly niacin and pyridoxine, B vitamins increase metabolic process and increase the energy levels and typical brain functions
. Take in food high in pyridoxine
. Take in food high in niacin
. Take in tons of vitamin C and bioflavanoids, increases energy and has antioxidant homes
. Eat fresh and raw vegetables and fruits as they supply anti-oxidants and flavanoids which help in decreasing swelling and improving up resistance
. Take in foods wealthy in vitamin E, increases blood circulation and safeguards brain cells
. Boost consumption of vitamin D.

Vitamins and Minerals

Minerals and vitamins recommened for narcoleptic clients are:
Omega-3 fat- membranes of cells in the body are made from special fats. Disturbance of their function impacts synthesis and secretion of neurotransmitters. Omega-3 fat is necessary to preserve the stability of cell membranes

Lecithin and L-Glutamine boosts psychological stability and awareness

Vitamins B, C, E and K are necessary anti-oxidants and body immune system modulators

Choline- is a substrate in the synthesis of acetylcholine. It is a neurotransmitter that contributes in sleep-wake cycle

Magnesium, selenium and chromium picolinate enhances blood supply to the brain and improves oxygen usage by the brain.

Chapter 3: Safe Treatment without Drugs

Narcolepsy treatment without drugs can even be practiced to help manage the signs. Here are some of them.

1. Sleep Cycle. Preparation shorts naps, for example, when done at routine periods can help promote your system for around 1 to 3 hours according to specialists. There are numerous apps that you can download nowadays to help track sleep cycle like FitBit One, Sleep as Android, Jawbone Up, iOS Sleep Cycle, and Sleepbot. With knowledge utilized from innovation, you can produce effective coping systems and begin leading a more regular life.

2. Vitamin Supplements. According to numerous research studies, tons of clients with narcolepsy are also identified to struggle with vitamin shortage. Vitamin D shortage is typically gotten in touch with strong pain and tiredness which, if not dealt with, can intensify one's circumstances. Increasing Vit. D by means of supplements just like that of NatureWise Vitamin D3 can offer extra 5,000 IU to the body for every single pill popped. Getting direct sunshine for several minutes also helps. Vitamin B12 through natural supplements or by taking in vitamin-rich foods can help promote the system and counter the signs.

3. Sweat it out. Light to moderate workout can help manage your signs but, if possible, do so with a friend or an individual trainer who comprehends your condition. Pilates, yoga, and walking are the most safe alternatives as you won't be using devices that might prove to be dangerous. Several minutes on a BodyBoss Home Fitness Center 2.0, for instance, can help accelerate your system and decrease other signs like brain fog and anxiety while boosting your muscle strength and versatility.

4. Omega threes. High quality natural supplement of omega-3 fats is also understood to help manage narcoleptic conditions just like ADHD in kids. You do not need to worry about its nasty after-taste as there are burpless natural supplements out there like the Dr. Tobias Omega 3 Fish Oil. A single pop can help enhance one's cognitive function and manage other signs. It is safe for kids and grownups in addition to pregnant and breast feeding ladies too.

5. Talk Treatment. Look for a support system or a therapists. Blurting your disappointments and learning reliable coping systems to manage your signs can help get rid of negative emotions functioning as stimulant for you to live life to the maximum. One crucial point in narcolepsy is anxiety as it can cause numerous other incapacitating signs. Striking anxiety at its core by means of talk treatment or getting associated with support system will help significantly in handling the condition.

6. Removal Diet plan. Aside from eating foods wealthy in minerals and vitamins, booting out foods that are understood to intensify the condition ought to be gotten rid of from your diet plan. Some of the foods understood to have heavy irritants are chocolate, wheat, soy, alcohol, caffeine and sugar-y products. These foods can unpredictably trigger disruption to your body and aggravate signs. Taking in a diet plan wealthy in vegetables and fruits, low fat dairy, entire grains and lean protein is highly suggested.

7. Alternative Treatments. Other recognized tried-and-tested treatments used by clients with narcolepsy are acupuncture; massage treatment, acupressure, and meditation can offer positive results. Aromatherapy using vital oils for massage or for diffusion can help improve sleep quality and eliminate stress and anxiety. Buying an aromatherapy diffuser like the InnoGear will help.

Certain Preventative measures
Narcolepsy has no recognized remedy approximately this day. The main point of narcolepsy treatment without drugs or artificial medication relies mainly on finding natural methods to manage the signs and keep a client safe from erstwhile dangerous activities when the condition strikes. As always, it is best to speak with your doctor right before diving into self-medication or natural treatment system to make sure security and sound health along with to eliminate certain medical conditions and issues that might come with it.

Natural Treatments for Narcolepsy

Cayenne Pepper
Capsicum Minimum is the Latin name of the herb. Cayenne Pepper is also referred to as Guinea spice or Cow Horn Pepper. It is called after a city in French Guiana called Cayenne. The fruit of the herb is squashed into a powder and used as a spice. This herb is also readily available in the form of tablets, casts and lotions. Cayenne Pepper enhances food digestion in addition to flow in the body.

Due to this, it is extremely beneficial for making an individual feel alert and active. For That Reason, Cayenne Pepper is a really good natural treatment for fending off extreme drowsiness brought on by narcolepsy. You can use Cayenne Pepper as a spice and also include it to hot beverages, soups or gravies and take in these to obtain the advantages of the herb.

Gotu Kola
Gotu Kola is a herb which has been used in Ayurveda for treating a lot of ailments. This herb is a moderate stimulant and it is great for triggering and stimulating an individual experiencing narcolepsy. Gotu Kola enhances the performance of the connective tissues in the body. This enhances the strength of the veins and boosts the flow of blood and nutrients to the brain.

Scientists really believe that this alters the sleep patterns of the brain and enhances an individual's activity levels throughout the day. Gotu Kola also oxygenates the brain. You can take this herb in an extract form for finest actual results.

Nation Mallow
Sida Cordifolia or Flannel Weed is some of the other names by which this herb is also understood. The seeds and roots of the herb are used to make different medications. Nation Mallow includes ephedrine which promotes and triggers the system. This helps to block the signs of narcolepsy like sleepiness throughout the day. You can use this herb to make tea which you should drink frequently to ward off narcoleptic signs. Nation Mallow does produce changes in high blood pressure in some cases. For that reason, individuals with cardiovascular conditions should only use this organic treatment after speaking with a medical professional and a herbalist.

Gingko Biloba
Gingko Biloba is a herb which triggers the nerve system and raises energy levels in people. This herb has been used thoroughly in conventional Chinese medication for some illnesses and health issue. Gingko Biloba enhances blood circulation in the body and helps in improving the supply of blood to the brain. It also consists of anti-oxidants which revitalize and invigorate the body. Terpenoids and flavanoids found in this herb are really reliable in recovering an individual who experiences narcolepsy. You can take this herb in supplement form or as an extract.

St. John's Wort
Hypericum Perforatum is the botanical name of the herb. This herb relaxes the nerves. It also improves the quality of sleep in the night. An individual struggling with narcolepsy gets in deep sleep without going through the phases of light sleep initially and might experience trouble in awakening throughout the day. But, St. John's Wort brings back typical sleep patterns to people who have narcolepsy, according to some specialists. St. John's Wort can be taken in the form of an extract. You can also make tea using the dried form of the herb and drink this regularly to experience its useful impacts.

Rosemary
Rosmarinus Officinalis is the botanical name by which this herb is also described. Rosemary is a well-known cooking herb. It is also used to deal with memory issues. Nevertheless, this herb has yet another usage. It can be used as a circulatory stimulant to make narcoleptic people alert and mindful throughout the day. Rosemary includes camphor which keeps the mind and body alert yet avoids overstimulation.

Rosemary also enhances the flow in the body and avoids daytime sleepiness face to faces detected with narcolepsy. You can include dried Rosemary to meals, soups and gravies and have these for enhancing your wakefulness throughout the day, if you experience narcolepsy.

Asian Ginseng

Panax Ginseng also called Asian Ginseng is a herb which has countless advantages. Among the lots of an identified of Ginseng is to deal with sleep conditions like narcolepsy. To get rid of disrupted sleep patterns throughout the night and day, individuals with narcolepsy can use Asian Ginseng. You can take 2 to 3 cups of Ginseng preparation daily. You can also take this herb in the form of an extract. Ginseng is also readily available in the form of a cast.

Asian Ginseng also referred to as Chinese Ginseng or Korean Ginseng also enhances flow and blood flow to the brain, which improves the capability of the person to get rid of severe drowsiness. Asian Ginseng is also taken in the form of tea, pills and powder. Do not use this herb if you struggle with high blood pressure too.

Guarana
Paullinia Cupana is the Latin name of the herb. It includes xanthine alkaloids just like caffeine which enhance the awareness and activity levels of individuals identified with narcolepsy. The seeds of the herb are used to make medication. This herb is also readily available in cast and pill form. Besides narcolepsy, this herb is also used for dealing with anxiety and psychological tiredness.
Guarana fend off the extreme drowsiness and propensity to wander off to sleep found in people who experience narcolepsy. This herb is also readily available in powder form. You can even roast the seeds of the herb and squash them to a great powder. Consume this frequently to get the advantages of the herb. Those who have high blood pressure issues need to not take this natural treatment.

Chapter 4: NLP Training

What Is Neurolinguistic Programming?

NLP, Neurolinguistic Programming is thought about a plan for the brain in the regards to assisting you accomplish your objectives. We are all taught mathematics, history and a host of other subjects, but we are never ever taught how to accomplish success, be a very happy efficient person or develop harmonize relationships. NLP can aid with these things.

NLP, Neurolinguistic Programming can teach you abilities that will help you use your brain and feelings to produce a life that succeeds and happy. This ability helps in your relationships with other individuals and increases your communication capabilities. The abilities learned will help you enhance how you believe, how you feel and how you behave. NLP is a broadening variety of knowledge with exceptional methods for accomplishing your life's objectives. NLP, Neurolinguistic Programming will also help you do whatever you do now better. NLP, Neurolinguistic Programming will also help you learn and master things you do refrain from doing now, but want to. You will also have the ability to believe more plainly, communicate better, manage your state of minds, ideas and habits quickly and efficiently.

Lots of people describe NLP, Neurolinguistic Programming as the research study of success, science of accomplishment, innovation of the mind. NLP is the research study of what makes one person effective and another person a failure. What NLP, Neurolinguistic Programming does is research study how effective people in all walks of life attain their success. NLP, Neurolinguistic Programming then takes the technique that you can model these exact same practices and strategies that they used to accomplish your own success. The net advantage of the model is it ends up being an incredibly highway to the specialist's success. You can learn in as low as couple hours what the specialists have taken years to learn.

NLP got its name from Richard Bandler and John Mill. The title happened as
Neuro - The connection that are between the body and mind through neural procedures.
Linguistic - Patterns of conduct and language that an individual has learned a lot from experience.
Programs - The shows describes experiences that are inscribed on every one of us.

NLP, Neurolinguistic Programming initially happened in the 1970's as a type of treatment that had the ability to deal with a broad location of issues that included anxiety, phobias, learning conditions and so on. NLP, Neurolinguistic Programming also exposed the capability for a private to highlight his real potential by conquering prior learned constraints. NLP, Neurolinguistic Programming also found that through its functions people developed a sense of well being and began working in a healthier manor.

Starting with NLP

Neuro-linguistic shows is an idea that you might or might not have heard about but finding out more about it could change your life. Neuro-linguistic shows or NLP is a system that checks out the characteristics between mind, language, and conduct in people. It is an approach of assisting human entities accomplish their finest self and is asserted on the simple fact that human experience is totally grounded in subjectivity. Let's take a much closer take a look at NLP to see precisely what it is really all about and how it can be helpful.

NLP was developed in the 1970's by John Mill, a linguist, and Richard Bandler, a therapist and mathematician. Their objective was to debunk the relationship between the mind and language and their affect on human conduct to help human entities accomplish happier, more grounded and efficient lives. Mill and Bandler actually believe that the neural system manages our bodies, language figures out how we communicate with other ones worldwide around us and our conduct is formed by the interaction of our beliefs, neural procedures and communication. A primary premise behind NLP is that if we can find positive methods to harness the power of the mind, language, and conduct we cannot only form better selves but also a much better world.

NLP is at its core a holistic method to comprehending the human. It acknowledges that everyone experiences the world subjectively and hence everyone has really special requirements for finding their course and attaining their finest self. The following are some of the primary objectives and goals of NLP:

Finding and developing the models that gives people the required tools to recover, change and become a state of quality
Assisting people explore their identity and their distinct purpose/mission in life
Assisting people face spirituality (the Meta level of human experience) and enabling them to develop their knowledge, instinct and vision.

One technique that NLP professionals use to satisfy the previously mentioned objectives and goals is hypnosis. Since NLP is rooted in the belief that the mind and language are what program and shape our reality, hypnosis is an outstanding approach of assisting people develops brand-new truths that are healthy and optimum for them as people. Hypnosis is a reprogramming of the mind to impact behavioral change and lots of hypnotherapists integrate the practice with the principles of NLP to help their clients make the needed changes to a better and more satisfying life, whether this means stopping smoking or arising out of a deep anxiety. A hypnotherapist with an NLP background can be the distinction between being stuck in the filth of old, self-defeating routines and the discovery of brand-new methods to view and be in the world in joy.

There are a lot of critics of the NLP model (and hypnotherapy for that matter) and they usually can be found in the form of traditional medical and mental specialists. Nevertheless, whether you really believe in NLP or hypnotherapy as practical techniques of treatment for different problems, they can never ever harm you physically or psychologically. Drugs, the approach of treatment most often promoted in mainstream medication, can have adverse effects and even be deadly. Hence, NLP and hypnotherapy are in the extremely least safe and this makes them worth having a look at if you feel that you really need to make some essential changes in your life. Mainstream thinking does not always have all the answers, and NLP is about finding the guts to acknowledge that and check out brand-new methods of thinking and being and for that reason it is well worth a much closer look.

The Science Behind It

Neuro-Linguistic Shows or NLP consists of the leading 3 dominant elements including the production of human experience. These are programs, language and neurology. Man's neural system determines how the body functions; language ascertains the way we communicate and user interface with other people; and, the human programs manages the kinds of world models that we develop. For this reason, NLP defines the standard characteristics amongst the human mind (Neuro) and the language people speak (linguistic) and how the interaction of these 2 impacts the body and its conduct (programs).

NLP was established in the 1970s by Richard Bandler and John Mill, declaring that it is necessary in looking for methods and means to help people to live fuller, richer and better lives. According to Bandler and Mill, NLP is a fast and most efficient kind of mental treatment, which can resolve an entire scope of issues that are very likely to be come across by psychologists, like anxiety, phobias, psychosomatic disease, practice condition and learning conditions. NLP also specifies that self-determination might be accomplished by hurdling learned constraints, and puts focus on healthy performance and general wellness. According to NLP's creators, any can learn abilities to boost their efficiency, both expertly and personally.

Who Uses NLP?
NLP has delighted in appeal in the field of psychology but it stayed neglected by standard science because of problems like absence of empirical proof, expert trustworthiness needed to validate the efficiency it said. In spite of being well-known, it barely made its presence felt in the field of scholastic psychology and mainstream therapy and psychiatric therapy.

Nonetheless, NLP was valued by personal psychotherapists - in addition to hypnotherapists - with some declaring to have been trained and are practicing NLP.

NLP Training has made rather an influence on management training, the self-help market and life training.

NLP is based upon 2 fundamental pre-suppositions:
1. The Map Does Not Translate Into Area. As we are human, we do not precisely know what reality is. Nevertheless, each of us views reality in different methods. Therefore, we react to stimuli surrounding us through sensory depictional categories. It is not reality itself which recognizes how we behave but, rather, our individual Neuro-linguistic charts of reality that does

- and which gives our conduct its meaning. It is not precisely reality which empowers or restricts us, but our maps or charts of reality.

2. Mind and Life Are Thought About Systemic Procedures. The procedures taking place within an individual and between other individuals and their scene are systemic. Our universe, societies and minds form environment comprised of complex systems together with sub-systems which interaction with and affect one another. It is unrealistic to completely separate a part of the system from the staying parts making up the system.

All the strategies and models of NLP are established on the synthesis of these 2 essential concepts. NLP says that ecology, knowledge and principles do not happen straight from one particular map of deep space, as man is not of developing. Instead, the objective is make the wealthiest map that acknowledges the ecology and systemic nature of people and deep space they reside in. The people who end up most reliable are those who have the ability to conceive a map of deep space which allows them to comprehend and view the most number of viewpoints and choices readily available to them.

How Does It Work?

NLP does not help you set objectives; an objective is pretty much up to a private to produce. NLP teaches a private to reprogram their reactions to their environment, providing a real chance to change their methods for solving issues. This in turn gives an individual a modification to attain objectives which, in the past, have run out reach.

The key to the efficiency of NLP is that it was developed by studying people who achieve success. By studying the pattern of actions, the thinking procedure, and choices of effective people NLP has developed strategies based upon real life circumstances. It is for this reason that Neurolinguistic Programming works.

Although it resembles psychiatric therapy, and lots of people consider it to be such, it is regularly considered life training. Whereas a therapist will try and repair a damaged person, so to speak, an NLP specialist will help a private learn abilities and strategies to attain objectives. An individual might wish to quit a bad practice like smoking or drinking. Another person might want to enhance their love life, and find a unique person to have a long term relationship with, but up previously has not been bring in the really wrong person. Others might want to make more cash, and attain greater monetary success. Some people are just looking for more joy but appear to be holding themselves back.

The essential strategy of NLP is what is called modeling. It takes a look at a person who has being successful in doing what you want to prosper at and after that copies the method that the effective person has used. Supporters of NLP really believe that if a single person can do something, then everybody else can do it too. The secret naturally, is to produce a design based upon what has worked for another person and after that execute this model. Changes might need to be made, and there is always a concentrate on what is working while disposing of aspects of a design that aren't working.

Unifying Mind And Body

Individual development can be attained through numerous methods. Among these is through the methods and techniques of Neuro-linguistic shows. The term Neuro-linguistic programs describes a group of strategies that are based upon the presumption that an individual's mind and language are adjoined and that this affiliation helps the person to connect to the world around him. Not only do the mind and language engage and relate, but an individual can impact his own conduct or other individuals' conduct by a method called "modeling.

According to the advocates of Neuro-linguistic programs, an individual can "model" his own conduct or another person's conduct so as to impact changes in those parts of his life that he feels less effective. If another person carries out exceptionally well on a job, then it is possible to learn that conduct. Neuro-linguistic programs includes methods like hypno-therapy which can possibly effect and change individual conduct.

Modeling as the Underlying Source of Neuro-Linguistic Programs
The body and mind engage with an individual's language to develop an understanding of the world. When this understanding or programs is malfunctioning, the person's emotions and responses are impacted and behavioral issues happen. Nevertheless, the person can be trained through neuro-linguistic shows methods, to copy or model certain conduct patterns from his own life which have succeeded and use them in regions in which he is not having. In the exact same way, an effective person's conduct and actions can be designed into a format that can be used to replicate his success in certain regions. The model is for that reason, changed into a habits pattern that cannot only be used by one but also taught to other ones.

Where Neuro-Linguistic Shows is The Majority Of Reliable
Neuro-linguistic programs might be used as a behavior modification by itself or in mix with other treatments and practices for individual development. It can be carried out through group sessions and workshops. Personal assessments between the specialist and the customer can also be used for effecting individual change through these approaches. The methods of neuro-linguistic shows can be used for more general concerns like eliminating certain phobias, conquering phase scare and ridding yourself of extreme negativeness that saps energy. Neuro-linguistic programs and modeling strategies are also useful to those with a history of dependency or anxiety.

More particularly, neuro-linguistic shows methods help those in the business and sporting fields to stand out at targets get higher levels of inspiration and handle communication problems. The concepts of the seriously well-known program are usually used for training and training specialists in different disciplines. In tons of businesses, it is used as part of the inspirational training program within the company, specifically in the fields of marketing and management training. In the more than 3 years since its beginning, neuro-linguistic shows has gone on to turn into one of the most reliable and commonly used tools for self enhancement. Although its strategies have not been properly investigated and verified, its appeal as a facilitator of individual development and objective achievement is self-evident.

The Advantages of NLP

Neuro-Linguistic Shows or NLP is really believed to be among the most effective and prominent ways that you can get people to actually believe you. Aside from the simple fact that it offers a methodical technique that can help you connect to an individual's inner mind, it can also produce positive change that you are certain to gain from. Whether you are a student, working grownup, business owner or retired person, you will also gain from it. Although there are still some people who think about NLP to be a scam, you will be astonished by what it can do, once you learn the appropriate way to use it.

In NLP, it is taught that language and conduct are highly structured and as such, they can be designed. Modeling is a technique where habits, language and beliefs of another person are gathered and integrated then created to a kind which can be taught to other ones. These models are taught and adjusted to individuals needing it.

NLP's Advantages Since its development in the 70s, Nero Linguistic Shows has already come a long way. The system has been used in so many numerous methods. Today, NLP is used in service, in health enhancement and even in sports.

In organisation, to be able to establish relationship with clients and customer is huge benefit. Even with a so-so item with a not so so-so cost, as long as a very good relationship is built between you and the customer, the result will rather agree with. NLP can enhance abilities in communication and management. It can also enhance management and inspirational abilities.

In sports, Neurolinguistic Programming can help you enhance in your game. It helps you focus on things and make you become more knowledgeable about the important things you're doing. If there's something really wrong it can be fixed immediately. For instance, a golf player who can't strike the ball correctly just because of his form would notice it and execute change. So the next time he hits a ball would be in correct form.

Healthcare can also gain from NLP. Positive thinking is an effective tool that can be used in the treatment and healing of clients. Neurolinguistic Programming can help develop clients develop the right mindset toward their condition and health problem. With a favorable outlook to their condition, it can produce enhancement.

NLP can also be used for your own individual advantage. Do you have a routine or a vice you want to stop? Do you want to stop smoking but it appears so tough? Neurolinguistic Programming can assist individuals with these types of issue. The system can also help in character enhancement.

Credibility of Neurolinguistic Programming NLP is a blend of science and art. A science since it utilizes different clinical approaches particularly in "modeling." It is an art as it handles people which are such vibrant entities.

Even with NPLs appeal and how it is being extensively used in different regions of life and by different specialists, it is still thought about to be outside the core of scholastic thinking.

Is it truly reliable or not? It depends upon the person under NLP. Some might declare it works some say it doesn't. But with the advantages Neurolinguistic Programming needs to provide without any negative effects, what have you got to lose if you try it.

Comprehending Neurolinguistic Programming is a way to guarantee life's success. NLP is a tested system and it can carry you toward the better life, if only you know how to use it appropriately. Do not opt for failures.

Methods That Will Change the Way You Believe

There are tons of neuro linguistic shows strategies that can benefit you on your journey of self enhancement. Although there are many strategies within NLP, I am going to share 3 essential techniques with you here today; modeling, reframing, and anchoring.

1. MODELING
NLP modeling is the procedure of duplicating quality. When you use modeling to attain success you really need to observe the conduct of a topic who has already attained that success. Concentrate on what the conduct is, how they do it, and why they do it; discover their underlying ideas. To put it simply find the ideas and beliefs that are hidden in the subconscious mind that enables them to reach their success. The key is to expose the ideas in their subconscious mind that are "different" from what other individuals are doing. Once you have determined the underlying ideas and beliefs, you will really need to develop a strategy or map of the steps needed to recreate their ideas, beliefs, and actions.

2. REFRAMING

Reframing is just one of the neuro linguistic methods that direct you in changing your understandings. It is a method that enables you to change the frame of an experience, event, or item. Reframing is a way to change the way you view something which in turn alters the method which you respond to it. For example, let's say you have an old batter trunk that is kept in the garage and is used for saving filthy shoes. You view that trunk as useless scrap. Then you learn that the trunk is actually worth a ton of cash. Your understanding has been reframed and you now take a look at the trunk with brand-new eyes. Reframing your understandings into positive ones gives you the capability to change how you deal with life.

3. ANCHORING

The 3rd method that will be gone over today is NLP anchoring. This method integrates connecting a trigger or anchor to a wanted feeling. An anchor is put in spot by choosing a trigger to mark the feeling. For example when you are in the preferred condition, like a state of complete peace, you can anchor that state by rubbing your hands together. Each time you get in that state of peace, rub your hands together to condition the anchor into your subconscious mind. The idea of anchoring is that once you anchor the trigger to the feeling you can generate that state of being when needed or wanted.

Obviously this is just a quick introduction of just a few of the neuro linguistic programs methods. In order to master NLP you really need to study the a lot of different strategies in a lot more detail. Comprehending this unbelievable field and executing it into your life will give you the capability to reach undeniable success.

Techniques

One's thought patterns, beliefs and mindsets can be used to "preprogram" real experiences that are yet to happen. NLP is extremely concentrated on how we believe, what affects the way we believe, and how we structure what we believe. Customers to the science are motivated to carefully study and after that model those people who do things well.

When studying them, you do not ask how they did it-just what they were thinking when they did it. For instance, if you asked Michael Jordan how to play basketball, he could give you a huge list of do's and do n'ts. He may lay out a series of needed drills, but that is not what NLP is about. Instead, you would discover how Michael Jordan views basketball in his mind. What are his beliefs and mindsets about basketball? When he decides on the court, what is he thinking?

NLP is comprised of some different models, each then having actually different strategies related to it. Let's break NLP down farther and take a fundamental take a look at some of its significant models.

Sub-modalities: The 5 Senses
Maybe the structure is, just enough, our 5 senses. Each of us takes in the world around us through our 5 senses: seeing, hearing, sensation (both concrete and psychological), tasting and smelling. Every little thing and anything we think of in life, and the resulting beliefs and mindsets we form, can be based upon what we get and after that analyze through these sub-modalities. Taking it a big step farther, with the totality of our life experiences encapsulated in our memories as we experienced them through our senses, we can recreate those experiences in our minds, modify them if requirement be and therefore acquire significant power over our idea patterns, beliefs and eventually the outside symptom of such through our abilities and accomplishments. The way you structure these likenesss in your mind identifies how you will react.

Try a fundamental experiment. Image somebody in your mind you hold extremely dear to your heart. Now, in your mind's eye, improve and magnify the colors of the image and observe how you react. What happens when you show up the volume of what has been said? What about if you imagine the image in tones of gray rather than color? For many people, "showing up" the colors or noises also heightens emotions, while turning them down decreases those emotions. Cultivating your capability to tweak the way you view things, or the way your mind represents things, can be used to make effective changes in your life. Once you recognize that you can, in essence, develop your world, you also recognize that you also have the power to change it.

Meta-Model
A meta-model is a set of questions that are developed for the particular purpose of finding the specific meaning in an individual's communication. For instance, typically when we communicate, we generalize, or we might even misshape info or leave it out altogether-intentionally or accidentally, purposely or unconsciously. People who use meta-models have the ability to methodically confirm and clarify both spoken and written communication to communicate much more plainly and exactly.

Sensory Skill
Our thought procedures are really carefully connected to our physiology. For instance, people can notice that you more than happy, terrified or upset without you even saying anything. Body movement sends strong hints about how we're feeling. That is, our posture, our eyes, our head position, and so on all say a lot about us. The majority of nonverbal communication is relatively apparent, but sensory skill takes these observations beyond the apparent and uses physical feedback in addition to spoken communication to be as critical as possible. Spoken hints even give some recommendation of which sensory method an individual runs from the majority of highly. For instance, if somebody says, "I hear what you're saying" versus "I see what you mean," it suggests that his/her acoustic sense is more dominant than his/her visual one. It is handy to give this principle consider since miscommunication can usually just arise from 2 people attempting to speak about the precise very same thing, only in different methods. Some specialists argue that if certain idea procedures are enhanced enough, over a long sufficient amount of time, they can actually modify an individual's physiological state.

Milton-Model

The Milton-Model, called after Milton Erickson, the dad of contemporary hypnotherapy, is a set of linguistic patterns that are developed to direct a person without actually interfering with the way s/he is experiencing the specific activity innerly. For instance, the command "Remember a time when you were sobbing" does not determine whether the person was sobbing frantically or weeping gently in the memory. This ability of defining emotions, spots, events and activities in a way that specifies and yet still universal permits the user to develop connection with his/her topic. It also helps move the topic into a trancelike state. As a result, the Milton-Model is typically used to cause hypnosis.

Meta-Programs

Meta-programs are basically the "looking glasses" through which we see the world. The traditional "Is the glass half full or half empty?" is a best meta-program example. Meta-programs control our character and for that reason how we behave. For example, do you tend to be more of an active or passive person? Do you focus more innerly or externally on the world around you? Is your orientation more concentrated on the past, the future or the here and now? 2 people might relate to the precise very same thing from completely different angles, to the degree that "specific very same thing" might actually become a really different thing entirely. For instance, do you move to your objectives, or do you move from the important things that aren't your objectives? One might just look like an inverted restatement of the other, but each has its own unique subtlety.

Conclusion

Persuasion is the really missing puzzle piece that will split the code to drastically increase your earnings, enhance your relationships, and help you get what you really want, when you really want, and win good friends for life. Ask yourself how much cash and earnings you have lost just because of your failure to encourage and affect. Think of it. Sure you have seen some success, but come up with the times you could not get it done. Has there ever been a time when you did not get your point right across? Were you not able to persuade somebody to do something? Have you reached your full potential? Are you able to inspire yourself and other ones to accomplish more and achieve their objectives? What about your relationships? Imagine having the ability to get rid of objections right before they happen, know what your prospect is thinking and feeling, feel more positive in your capability to encourage. Expert success, individual joy, management potential, and earnings depend upon the capability to convince, affect, and inspire other ones.

Self-confidence

When introducing NLP neuro linguistic programs it is crucial to take a minute and believe a part of your life where you might be positive. With that moment ask yourself this question: how do you know that you are proficient at, name that location? Now that you are being totally truthful with yourself, provide that answer. If you definitely know that you are great or skilled in that specific location you chose since your own idea or sensation or perhaps your belief told you so, that's where you really need to be.

If you were uncertain about your specific location or if you needed to depend on external verification from your peers, partner, or you aren't rather yet as positive as you can be. By that time you inform yourself with NLP, you will be right on point. You will also have the real self-confidence that originates from within when your finished with neuro linguistic programs methods.

Introducing NLP neuro linguistic programs for self-confidence, or absence thereof. This is a truth right across a lot of areas. Throughout all financial levels, all races, there will always be some people who are positive and some people who are not. With there being lots of NLP methods that really need to be learned, the huge bulk of people at this moment really believe that they are confident.NLP will show lots of the skills and the self-confidence to make things happen.

Now introducing NLP neuro linguistic programs to you and your family was actually without a doubt, a great advantage. One neuro linguistic shows strategy that is rarely written things about originates from ability development. It is called unconscious skills. This is the best phase of any ability. It is the state at which an ability has been instilled in the brain, resulting into what is referred to as a practice. You would no longer need to spend your time thinking of using that specific ability. People who are the best at what they do work at the greatest level of unconscious proficiency every day. If somebody were to inquire about how particularly they perform at such high levels, they most likely would not have the ability to define it verbally. The reason for this is that they are no longer mindful of what they are carrying out in order to perform at such high levels.

One last thing when choosing NLP is self-confidence contractors. Self-confidence contractors consist of several words; these words communicate a message saying that there is definitely no doubt in my mind that this is the manner in which it is. For instance: you will find words like definitely, absolutely certainly, or perhaps undoubtedly and naturally and sure. Introducing NLP neuro linguistic shows will implant these self-confidence contractors into your life and your vocabulary extremely rapidly.

NLP has been adjusted by a lot of therapists as a way of assisting people become mindful of what they tell themselves about their character and conduct. In essence, specialists of neuro linguistic programs strategies try to help people learn to stop self-defeating ideas and change with positive self-talk. This in turn is organized into helpful conduct patterns that enhance the positive inner discussion and focus on enhancing social interactions at the exact same time.

Although some researchers tend to discount rate NLP methods, lots of personal psychotherapists have included it into their restorative practices. NLP has had its largest impact in the fields of in self-help programs, life training and management training. In these parts neuro linguistic shows strategies are being practiced as approaches of attaining quality in efficiency.

Amongst the more well-known of neuro linguistic programs methods:

Connection. NLP suggests that to acquire connection with other individuals, there are advantages to matching one's own non-verbal conduct, just like posture, intonation, head position and so on, with another person. Some methods presume regarding motivate matching speech and body rhythms of other ones to attain shared connection.

Anchoring. This NLP procedure includes associating a specific reaction with a special stimulus, or anchor. A gesture, an intonation or a particular touch frequently are used as anchors, though an anchor could be any distinct sensory stimulus. Neuro linguistic programs advocates say this method looks like classical mental conditioning.

Reframing. In neuro linguistic shows methods, reframing includes providing an interaction component in a way that changes how a private sees the significances connected to words, expressions or events. The theory is that changing the understanding of the event results in changing the reactions and habits connected with the event too. Fairy tales, myths, legends and even jokes regularly use reframing as an interactions method.

Neuro linguistic programs strategies are now extensively used in tons of types of treatments and self-improvement techniques.

For Company

Online marketing practices have been progressing for several years now. The techniques employed till now include making use of SEO, blogging, social networking sites and a lot of other tools which have succeeded to a big level. The practice of neuro linguistic shows (NLP) can also be used for developing a connection with people who are online. Neuro linguistic programs describes an innovation which focuses on the conduct of people. It helps people to take control of their conduct and also identifies properly of reacting to a specific circumstances. The principle of neuro linguistic programs was introduced by John Mill and John Bandler in 1970.

The principle is about the distinction between an individual's reality and the person's understanding of the reality. For that reason, a lot depends upon your understanding of your own online company. This technique ought to not be puzzled with "controlling people to your benefit", since it is not so. There are persuasion methods which form part of NLP and this can be used for service functions. But eventually, the prospect preserves awareness and has 100% control of their actions.

NLP persuasion strategies can be used to draw in the right type of people to your site and toward your other online promos. The NLP methods make the most of effective behavioral patterns of site visitors. Depending upon the constant profile of the visitors, the language or images on your site can be changed according to their choices. For example, if you have a furnishings site and dream to bring in a specific group of consumers, maybe from the more wealthier class, the look of your site can be changed to show this choice. It is simple to develop an expert looking site once you know the kind of visitor you are attempting to encourage. The right sort of people would find it incredibly luring and can connect to such visual images and ideas presented on the site if you know to use NLP strategies successfully.

The essential element of NLP includes the research study of the profiles of your site visitors in detail, and after that creating the proper content to better affect their actions.

Comprehending their constant conduct is going to be of utmost value. This leads you to producing persuasion patterns over a time period. Another element of NLP strategies that works in site creation is anchoring. Anchoring is a method of gradually orienting the visitor's perspectives in a way that they become likely to purchase your product and services you are offering. For example, if you have a car parts site, then you can deal with common car concerns of the visitors to begin with. Then you can communicate how thinking in your services and products and in turn in your brand name, can benefit them.

Advanced NLP abilities consist of relating the services and products of your online organisation in a way that the visitor feels that they can't live without them. This can bring a brand-new measurement your marketing strategy if used efficiently.

The fundamental aim of using NLP strategies is to produce a wanted sense of responsiveness. After certain number of days on your interaction with your visitor, you should have the ability to move from the info phase to selling phase. Using neuro linguistic programs techniques can help you obtain from one phase to the next in a fast and effective way.

When creating your very first site, it is necessary to be familiar with the precise methods of NLP and how to use it into your site so that you can effectively affect visitors to take the actions you 'd like them to. Introducing NLP neuro linguistic shows into the graphics and content can dramatically enhance your conversion rates.

NLP and Hypnosis

Several years ago management theorists tried to use neuro theory and neuro linguistic shows to boost their company. NLP can aid with these things. NLP is also among the best methods to handle individual issues and to develop yourself. It is a broadening variety of knowledge with exceptional methods for accomplishing your life's objectives.

What NLP does is research study how effective people in all walks of life attain their success. It is also a brand-new and considerable branch of psychiatric therapy. Apart from that, it is a design of an alternative technique to psychiatric therapy and social interactions. In the years to follow, neuro linguistic shows will certainly get more motivation.

Also, Neuro linguistic Programs plays a major role in enhancing your psychological ideas. It's not a surprise that we can learn a lot about real pain relief and phobias through NLP itself. Anchoring is just one of the techniques of NLP that you can begin using today to change your way of life. Nevertheless, there still stay some debates connected to the basis or the nature of NLP methods.

NLP has already helped countless people conquer worries, boost self-confidence, improve relationships, and attain greater success.

The cousin of NLP is Hypnosis
Hypnosis is neither safe, nor is it hazardous. While efficient self-hypnosis takes practice, success brings the benefit of strong pain decrease. Self-hypnosis can be used for relaxation and tension decrease, for support and more inscribing of self-suggestions, and for ideomotor self-analysis.

Hypnosis and self-hypnosis are used to rapidly assist in behavioral changes without the requirement for self-control. There are types of hypnosis understood and experienced as day-dreaming and self-hypnosis. Self-hypnosis is safe and con-venient, has no negative side ef ¬ fects and can accompany and enhance other kinds of treatment. Emotive treatment, or behavior modification, or options- oriented treatment, for instance, in addition to hypnosis to give the clients' maximum advantages.

Some kinds of hypnosis focus upon treatment, while other kinds of hypnosis focus upon the art of persuasion. The reason phase hypnosis is not linked to the art of persuasion is since phase hypnosis needs volunteers. Phase hypnosis is a type of home entertainment hypnosis. Conversational Hypnosis is a procedure just like typical hypnosis or direct style hypnosis. One style of hypnosis is not better than another style of hypnosis. Hypnosis treatments are usually used to manage bedwetting, in hypnosurgery, to improve weight reduction, lower dependencies, and control conduct.

With this brand-new standard knowledge of hypnosis and NLP, you can start to check out each field to use it for your service.

Breaking Devoid Of Negative Ideas

How Negative Thinking Can Impact United States
Negative attitude impacts us not just mentally, but physically. Undoubtedly, negative ideas have real implications beyond just the thought itself. How can you use neuro linguistic shows and hypnosis to break without this?

Neuro linguistic shows is a method by which you can actually be taught to "re-train" the way you believe. Simply put, a therapist trained in NLP can help you rephrase and reiterate ideas, and consider them in a completely different light, so that you actually start to believe in different ways in which are more well balanced and positive - and certainly, more practical.

This is a really positive step to take because so usually, negative ideas are things that are "out of context" from what is actually going on.

Negative Thinking in Every Day Circumstances
Let's say for instance that you have been appointed a project at work, and you're positive you can do it. You finish the job and you have done well. Nevertheless, you see one small mistake. Immediately, you start to speak with yourself adversely, telling yourself that you dealt with the job inadequately, although the one small mistake is not considerable and will not influence on the quality of the task in general. So while your boss is saying, "Great job." you may be saying to yourself, "No, it's not. I'm so silly. I'm going to lose my job just because of that error."

How sensible is that?
A competent NLP Specialist might challenge you with this: "So, your boss has told you're going to lose your job since you made one little error?" How will you respond? You'll believe, "Obviously not." and recognize that your boss is telling you that you have done a great job. For that reason, neuro linguistic shows actually teaches us how to re-train our ideas in a more well balanced and positive style, based upon an unbiased examination of the real situations.

Now, what does this mean in regards to how you can keep away from following this pattern overall? Well, naturally, you take a big step back and take a look at the job with unbiased eyes. Objectively speaking, without that negative self-talk, you can see that really, you did a great job and made one little error. And although you plainly want to stay away from making errors, they do happen.

So a reasonable restatement of your preliminary response - that you managed the job inadequately - may be to say, "I did a great job and made one little error. I will take note next time and try not to make the exact same error, but I can still take pride in what I did however."

You can also tell yourself that since your boss mores than happy with what you did, you should not only take pride in what you have done, but you can be safe and secure that your job is safe. This is, in simple fact, what is sensible and present, and is a lot more precise as self-talk than your prior declaration.

Parenting and NLP

Parenting has been going on since the start of humankind, but lots of mom and dad still feel they need to transform the wheel over and over again and rely on some strange impulses they are supposed to have. Parenting is at initially a physical obstacle, then gradually; it changes into a psychological difficulty. Nevertheless it is highly preferable that mom and dad do use child-centered, non-directive play, as a part of their parenting activities. This needs unique Parenting Abilities.

For many individuals, parenting their kids is just one of the most satisfying emotions in their life. Parenting ability is really all about understanding your parenting character. This is very important as it helps you find how your character encourages the way you behave as a moms and dad and how your kid's character communicates with your own. As times have changed - parenting has ended up being more refined and some parenting abilities and strategies are readily available to make the procedure easier and less demanding. Below is just one of the most efficient and modern parenting ability; that can give you complete parenting fulfillment?

Neuro-Linguistic Parenting (NL Parenting) is a parenting ability that takes the essence of NLP and applies it to parenting scenarios. Very first let us comprehend what is NPL? NLP is the research study of how people know what they believe they know and how they do what they do (instead of 'why' they do what they do). NLP procedures can be used to check out beliefs. NLP checks out the relationships between the way we believe (Neuro), the way we communicate (Linguistic) and our patterns of conduct (Programs). Our minds, bodies, feelings, beliefs, knowledge and memories are all present and active concurrently. NEURO is our "Nerve system" through which experience is gotten and processed through the 5 senses. LINGUISTIC is our language and nonverbal communication systems through which neural depictions are coded, ordered, and given meaning. PROGRAMS is the pattern of symptom of our neural codes and communication.

NL Parenting is the parenting ability with a primary objective of dissemination of the essential procedures and info to help father and mother in attaining individual congruence. It is really all about creating choices from which we can choose, so it is the finest system we have for learning how to associate with kids in creative and in agreement methods. NLP in Parenting helps cultivate better communication between moms and dad and kid.

NL Parenting works quicker with kids and teenagers just since their nerve system is still in the procedure of incorporating those inner messages so they can be helped to erase and change them quicker. From an NL Parenting perspectives the roles of a moms and dad are; to control contexts so that kids can learn or play in relative security and to model or show extraordinary conduct and congruence. NL Parenting is the parenting ability which offers mother and father with a structure that helps their kids to work well with other ones and at the same time make parenting a satisfying experience.

We are typically surprised with the way our kids change their conduct when moving from one phase of their life to another and even within their individual life phases. Our 11 years of age kid who depended on us for all choices all of a sudden ends up being independent by the time they cross 13. Our baby who was groaning several minutes ago is smiling and laughing away now. Kids are professionals at changing states. The initial step to developing NL Parenting Ability is to comprehend the state of our kid. It is a lot like putting yourself in the shoes of your kid and comprehending how they believe, their requirements, what is driving their conduct (great or bad) and what are their disappointments.

This parenting ability can be accomplished by anchoring - which means associating their present state with their beliefs and surrounding. So if your 3 years of age understands that by creating a temper tantrum they will get what they really want, you really need to comprehend that creating a temper tantrum to have their way is the belief that your kid has developed. If you put yourself in their shoes, you will have the ability to indicate different circumstances where they have got a much better of you simply because you gave into their temper tantrum. These circumstances were the essential to development and support of their beliefs. It is really essential to keep in mind that although you feel that creating a temper tantrum in this circumstances is bad conduct - your kid certainly sees it as providing advantages. For this reason there is an incongruence of your beliefs versus your kid's.

Understanding their belief and comprehending the physical stimulus for the exact same is the 2nd step to getting NL Parenting ability. Nevertheless, anchoring is not the end of the procedure. By anchoring you will now have the ability to recognize the beliefs and the physical stimulus that you want to change. So the objective of the very first 2 steps is not to leave the state the same, but to find a way to change it that maintains some components of its advantages. So if your kid has created a temper tantrum to have a chocolate, you can try and work out with them to finish their supper initially and after that enable them to have a chocolate - such that you get some advantages out of the circumstances.

The last step of NL Parenting ability is the procedure of accomplishing irreversible change in your kid. Here training abilities play a really crucial role. Training comes in when a circumstance emerges that shows a space between, what the environment is asking and what abilities the kid might do not have. Training abilities give mom and dad the tools to build on their relationship with their kid and to produce chances for brave discussions. Obtaining the right training abilities is very important as it helps father and mother to determine their governing worths and requirements, which develops the basis of their parenting choices.

It helps to change your awareness about your kid's conduct, it stimulates your kid's successes, that promote wanted conduct and it recognizes & develops qualities that would not have otherwise existed. So in the prior example , through training mom and dad can produce a total different external stimulus for the kid - like say requirement for healthy teeth - and guide them from requiring chocolates and creating temper tantrum for them all the time.

Finally NL Parenting ability does not recommend any single parenting ideology, but determines models of parenting quality and abilities and strategies that advance us to more mild and considerate parenting. It helps you to acknowledge your parenting strengths, weak points and beliefs and permits you to become a real guide and coach to your kid.

End Up Being a Better Speaker with NLP

If a single person can be a spontaneous effective speaker, so can other ones. Speaking strongly is a threefold procedure: Using one's body to enter a positive state, stopping stress and anxiety develop, and running the film in your mind that YOU ARE CONFIDENT.

Usage of Body: Our Mind and body interact. In other words, the body is the hardware and the brain is the software application. For an individual to feel great and become an effective speaker, the very first element to master is the 'Mindful usage of body'. The body needs to send out positive signals to the brain in regards to its well being- A strong position: head straight, put up shoulders, equivalent weight on both feet; sluggish and deep breathing (also called 'Stomach Breathing') gives a strong signal to the mind about the convenience level. It establishes the brain for positive thinking mode, as the body has supplied its consent. When was the last time you saw an individual with saggy shoulders, head down, and shallow breathing providing an effective speech?

Getting rid of stress and anxiety related to public speaking: The worry connected with public speaking is normally just because of Stress and anxiety. To comprehend how an individual develops stress and anxiety is really crucial. Each person is different, and will have a very different experience while experiencing stress and anxiety. For instance: An individual may imagine having butterflies in his/her stomach, most likely a picture of him/her with people chuckling in that scene, which he/her can even hear.

To get rid of stress and anxiety, try evaluating the sub-modalities (in other words characteristics) of the origin: Instructions of spin of butterflies in the stomach, quality of the image (mainly negative in this case - dark, without borders etc). An easy resolution like reversing the direction of butterflies, and making the dark image with people chuckling a colored one with borders, and misshaping the noise of people chuckling into a duck quacking can change the mind pattern and aid getting rid of the stress and anxiety.

Positive belief: To produce self-confidence, all that is needed is to close your eyes and return in your past and get connected with the memory when you were incredibly positive in an offered circumstances. Notification the sub-modalities of the senses (visual, acoustic, kinesthetic, olfactory, and gustatory): You might have the ability to see colored bright images, hear loud sound of people clapping, feel heat in your body, and so on. Know these sub-modalities and increase the strength of these characteristics in your mind to increase your self-confidence producing characteristics. Take the sub-modalities of self-confidence of that specific circumstances and use it to public speaking with see an impressive distinction.

Weight Reduction with NLP

If you are having a hard time to make development with a weight-loss program, or if you are just thinking about starting one, you might want to follow these 5 suggestions thoroughly. You might have the ability to attain your weight-loss objectives much faster and in a simple and relaxed way if you follow the 5 suggestions about: Designing Quality, Mindset, Interest and Confusion, Change, and Having A Good Time along the Method.

The acronym NLP represents Neurolinguistic Programming. The analysis of the name is as follows: Neuro represents anything relating to brain and nerve system in general. Linguistic refer to language or our spoken or otherwise analysis of experiences. Finally, Shows represents forming of brain circuitry patterns or beliefs. NLP handle grasp of our capability to change the anxious, linguistic and programs patterns to enhance our communication with ourselves and other ones and to enhance the total quality of our lives.

Let us go right into the 5 weight-loss ideas based upon the NLP concepts:

Designing Quality: It is great when you have a strong belief in what you are doing from the beginning. If you are thinking about purchasing a weight-loss item or signing up with a weight reduction program, make certain you know it is originating from an outstanding source. If you do not at this time know much about the source, usage web to learn more. Empower yourself by developing that weight-loss item or program even right before you purchase. NLP actually believes every little thing another person can do you can do too. So check out all reviews you can get your hands on. Ask your good friends if they know anybody who had success. An exemptional model for instance to follow is great to have right before you even begin.

Mindset: In NLP, Mindset comes first. Right before beginning a weight-loss program make certain to check your mindset. Yes, NLP states every little thing somebody else can do you can learn and do also. Nevertheless, you need to simplify into little portions first. Know that there are specifics you will learn along the way that you have not the slightest idea about at this moment. Know there may be barriers to get rid of that you know absolutely nothing about at this time. Handle the can-do mindset initially when you begin. Although you can acknowledge it, do not concentrate on your present weight. Instead, imagine yourself already well on your way to slimming down already, and that is simply because of your mindset.

Interest and Confusion: Interest and confusion will work in your favor. Throughout your very first days and weeks dealing with your brand-new program, a weight reduction diet plan, or a weight reduction workout program, or some other routine, you will likely experience a state of interest. You will ask yourself, "I really wonder how this program will work for me?", or "What changes will I experience initially?" Other times you will experience confusion: "Why is this not working for me as it was supposed to?" Both interest and confusion are great indications. They both take you from your typical and accustomed methods of thinking into the brand-new, more versatile and broadened methods. And, as a great hypnotherapist once said, "Knowledge is always preceded by confusion."

Modification: It is really up to you to change. Using NLP, there is no requirement anymore to stay stuck in a down spiral leading you from a bad circumstances to an even worse circumstances. No requirement to repeat the thinking and the conduct that got you here in the very first spot. Therefore, no requirement to harp on the past. It is fine to acknowledge the past and that is all. Rather than home on the past, focus your ideas and language on the positives that you expect will come. Stay open up to change; change can be made satisfying and successful.

Have a good time Along The Way: This is a huge suggestion. There is an abundance of possible results in your weight reduction mission. Also there is an abundance of the methods to get where you want to be. So why not choose a manner in which is both fun and reliable with your weight reduction objectives. It being fun will help you stick to your activities. And, please, do not take yourself too seriously. It is far better to take your activities seriously. Or to make certain you have serious fun doing them. And it is fine to be serious about your objectives. But you aren't flawless now and you will not be flawless when you have shed your pounds either. So brighten up on the severity about yourself and enjoy your trip.

Techniques to Re-Program Your Mind

A ton of people feel discouraged since they believe they can't focus, they can't learn or they can't be successful. Well, there is great news. You can configure yourself for success, to focus more and to learn simpler if you use the right neuro linguistic programs methods that people throughout the world have used and offered to all of us.

The following are 3 techniques that you can use to configure your mind for success through making use of neuro linguistic programs methods.

The number 1 technique to set your mind for success is tips and self-suggestions. This is when you are at a hypnosis center and the hypnotherapist comes, help you unwind your body and give you recommendations. Or self-suggestions is you, speaking to yourself and giving recommendations to your subconscious mind. Tons of neuro linguistic shows methods can help you go through that procedure.

The 2nd technique to set your mind for success is by utilizing visualizations. Imagining what you really want is effective. If you can't envision it and develop psychological photos in your mind, just draw images of what you really want. Cut images in publications or paint your desires if you really want. Then you can concentrate on these images so they can stick in your mind. That's one way of picturing, for those that declare that they can't picture. Lots of neuro linguistic programs methods can help you master visualization.

The 3rd technique to configure your mind for success is what is called brain entrainment. Brainwave entrainment tools and CDs produce and produce specific brainwaves to get you into the state that you really want: imagination, focus, relaxation ... Essentially, rather than going to costly workshops and training to learn how to perform auto-hypnosis, you can listen to a brainwave entrainment CD that will get you into that flawless frame of mind that you prefer when you want it.

If we thoroughly follow a couple of those approaches mentioned above, you will recognize that we can be able to focus, learn and be successful. Certainly using the above suggested programs or techniques will enable yourself to attain your objectives and to help you enhance yourself in a way that you never ever thought you can. In addition, always remember that success is not done over night, always keep in mind that you really need to go through these techniques to guarantee yourself of being on the right track and direction. Take one step at a time, and you will never ever be at loss as you enhance yourself.

Controlling Inspiration and Beliefs

NLP analyzes our feelings, and asks us to believe more thoroughly about why these feelings are occurring. If we feel mad, or upset, happy or miserable, it might appear apparent regarding why the reason. We then go on and try and repair this issue as finest we can. The issue is, in some cases we misread our psychological signals, overlook them, or cover the real reasons behind why we feel that way.

Inspiration plays a vital part in Neuro-linguistic programs principals. It is definitely the case that people move toward satisfying experiences, and way from the uncomfortable. We, though, are somewhat lazy in this regard - short-term results will usually take precedence over the long term. For instance, everybody understands that if they work out, then they will eventually feel better, be more powerful, and have more energy. The inspiration is nevertheless, not always there, as we do not feel any short-term advantages (and even feel short-term real pain and pain). On the other hand, we know that eating a chocolate bar will lead to us being unhealthier and maybe fatter in the future, but the short-term gain is too appealing.

Neuro-linguistic programs takes the inspiration behind our actions really seriously, and among the primary principals of the strategy is learning how to take control of inspiration. NLP can help one concentrate on the long term advantages of an action rather than the instantaneous buzz of a short-term repair.

Neuro-linguistic programs says that we, as people, start to develop beliefs about the world in which we live, and we use these beliefs to govern our choices and conduct. The majority of the time these follow apparent reasoning (e.g. fire is hot, do not put your hand in a fire), but in some cases negative beliefs can be developed (e.g. do not ask anybody out, as you will always be turned down). These negative beliefs can originate from a single interaction or an occasion in one's life that starts to manifest itself and become extremely popular in an individual's mind.

NLP is really all about breaking these patterns, by giving people the tools to acknowledge their conduct, their beliefs, their inspirations and their worries. Once one has the ability to see in what methods one's beliefs might be inaccurate or damaging, NLP methods can help break these negative habits, and change them with efficient and helpful habits.

Financial Health.

Do you know people who always appear to do well economically, and other ones who are always having a hard time no matter the financial times? What produces this distinction in reality experience?

In general people do not question their experience of reality. It is the ground we base on to understand our world. It just is what is. Truth is what we see, experience, and feel. We experience it as something goal that is external to us, and that enforces itself on us.

But we are never ever experiencing reality straight. We are only experiencing a design of reality. That is since we specify reality based upon the info that our senses are getting. But there are enormous quantities of info that are bombarding our senses every moment, and it would be unrealistic to take all of it in. So we filter in a really little portion of it, and filter out the majority of it. What we filter in or out is really subjective, relating to the operations of our mind. But it is what specifies our model of reality. This means, to a big degree and on an unconscious level, we are picking our experience of reality, instead of reality enforcing itself on us.

Restricting choices can have a lot to do with what pieces of info you filter in or out. From the NLP perspectives, restricting choices are what trigger you to bring into your life what you do not really want, instead of what you do really want - like monetary battles instead of monetary health. They are at the core of what keeps in spot any pattern in your life that is not working well.

They are choices just like you are bad, not important, helpless, that people can't be relied on, and so on. Restricting choices are generally formed right before the age of 6 or 7 years of age, and in some cases in teenage years.

Here's an example of a restricting choice being formed from the Neurolinguistic Programming perspectives:

Let's say you are 5 years of age. Your dad normally gets back from work really late each night, looking tired from working so hard. He's always too worn out and irritable to have fun with you and just wants everybody to be silent. But this night he gets home from work early, looking mad and beat. He has just been laid off from his job. You can tell he just wants to forfeit. And your mom looks really scared.

You all of a sudden feel extremely overloaded, scared and insecure. You find yourself in an inner state of mayhem and confusion, as you have never ever experienced this type of circumstances previously. It's a state of shock. The psychological procedure that usually happens for kids when this sort of thing takes place is that your mindful mind stops operating, and your unconscious mind takes control of. This is a really impressionable hypnotic trance state. In this state you choose a importance for what you have just experienced.

Let's say in this case you choose that prospering in life is a frustrating battle. And after that choice gets locked into your physiology - your contraction, your breathing patterns and your neuro-networks. Then you mindful mind reclaims over, not seeing your unconscious mind has decided. And after that, you're filtering your experience through that choice, like an unconscious presumption about the nature of life. Simply put your experience of reality has now been misshaped, just because of that choice. And your unconscious mind then ends up being really bought showing that choice is really true. In order to do that it works like a background computer system program, filtering in info that shows the restricting choice to be real, and removing info that negates it.

You have now created an inner reality that prospering in life is a frustrating battle. And how you approach earning money as you grow up will play out this reality. No matter what you do, or what sort of job you search for, you always find yourself having a hard time economically. Or maybe you be successful for a while, but ultimately you fall back into the exact same sort of having a hard time monetary state.

You might ultimately recognize that life does not need to be that way, as you observe other ones doing far better than you. You might study the Law of Attraction and go to wealth workshops and try any number of things to learn how to prosper in company. But you find yourself essentially knocking your head against the wall. And that is since you aren't handling the source of the issue, which is in your unconscious mind. That's where the restricting choice is secured.

The NLP TimeLine Process is a really efficient resolution to launching restricting choices that hold monetary or practically any sort of issue in spot. Through hypnosis, this procedure brings you back to that really first event in which you made the restricting choice, so as to launch it from your unconscious mind. As it uses Neurolinguistic Programming innovation, it is established according to how the brain develops experience, and is really efficient at effecting extensive life change.

Chapter 6: Acupuncture

The History of it

Acupuncture is a conventional Chinese medication that goes back some 10,000 years. It is a strategy used to promote trigger points in the body by the usage of needles to help reduce real pain and deal with different illnesses.

Files show that the practice started throughout the Stone-Age period, where sharp-edge stones and tools are used to pierce and deal with abscesses. Then later, the strategy progressed to using needles made from metals just like gold, silver, and bronze.

The viewpoint of acupuncture is rooted from the mentors of Taoism. It promotes the balance of yin and yang by getting consistency between the body and its environments. The very first book that was put together with a system of medical diagnoses and treatment about acupuncture is the Classic of Internal Medication book of the Yellow Emperor, dating between 100 BC and the very first AD. The text revealed assistance of the Taoist viewpoint and handed-down conventional medications over the centuries.

It also developed accurate physiological places of the meridians, or the Qi energy or essential vital force that streamed within the body. Initially, there were 365 pressure points that were representing the days of the year. The book also defines the beginning of different illnesses, and what acupoints should be used to treat them.

Years later, acupuncture went on to develop and was gradually introduced to different parts of the world, consisting of Europe and the United States. It ended up being the basic treatment in China, together with making use of herbs, moxibustion or making use of heat treatment, diet plan, and massages.

Another substantial turning point of acupuncture was throughout the Ming Dynasty where they formed the brand-new basis of the treatment. Ming ordered to cast a bronze statue marking all the 365 pressure points, which was used for cross referral. They also released a book about the success of acupuncture and moxibustion method, which was consequently used by future dynasties. Aside from showing the different pressure points, the book also includes safety measures of the 2 strategies and what adjustment method is best used.

Acupuncture was promoted thoroughly when Sun Simiao, a distinguished doctor from the Tang Dynasty, put together another book for the medical experience of acupuncture. He produced a chart of 3 views, a various colored chart of all the channels throughout the body. It was then that acupuncture was thoroughly accepted by the masses, and its usage was extensively spread out. And ultimately, the number of pressure points grew to 2,000 from 365.

Medical Exchanges of Acupuncture

The spread and exchange of acupuncture began when China sent their doctors to different nations, consisting of Korea, Japan, and the European nations. They held regular workshops and lectures, and shared a variety of books to promote all Chinese Medication.

Between the 500 A.D. and 700 A.D., China introduced acupuncture to Japan. They presented copies of books about acupuncture classics and value of acupuncture points. Through this, the Japanese federal government passed a law in 702 A.D. to completely study acupuncture and use it as their source of medication.

The spread reached Korea in 1092, where the exchange of doctors and strategies was extremely widespread. The science behind acupuncture was also distributed through other nations, like India in the early 6th century. And it was only throughout the 16th century, when Europe accepted the advantages of acupuncture.

Nevertheless, interest for acupuncture decreased throughout the 17th century as it was actually believed to be an illogical medication. This produced the intro of western medications, but the knowledge and practice stayed in main China.

The appeal of acupuncture started in the United States only in the 19th century when an author from the New york city Times produced a short article on how acupuncture brought remarkable remedy for his persistent real pain. He was astonished how acupuncture gave him a more extended relief, far from the anesthesia and pain relievers he was taking.

Though acupuncture is not thought as exceptional to western medication, it is now extensively accepted and really believed to be reliable. It is a holistic treatment that doesn't concentrate on the precise reason for any condition or disease. Rather, it patterns its treatment from the negative imbalances that the body endures caused by its mind, way of life, external pathogens, environment, and stress factors.

It uses 12 meridian channels, which they actually believe is where our "Qi" or energy circulations. And by placing needles, these channels are promoted, and the body is reminded its balance. Research studies even show that acupuncture treatments can increase pain-relieving hormonal agents, just like serotonin and endorphins that block real pain experience and swelling. Acupuncture also shows to enhance blood flow and the body immune system. Certainly, acupuncture is no longer an old practice, but a holistic treatment shown to deal with a large range of conditions and illnesses.

The Possible Advantages

Acupuncture is a kind of conventional Chinese medication that uses using unique 'hair-thin' needles that are placed just right below the skin at tactical points in the body referred to as "acupuncture points". This helps in controlling the flow of energy, promotes the body's recovery systems, reduces strong pain and brings back health in myriad methods.

Acupuncture Boosts Fertility
Ladies getting IVF treatment can increase their chances of getting pregnant by 50% if they get the right acupuncture treatment.

Acupuncture Lowers Your Variety Of Headaches
Rather than stockpiling on aspirin, Acupuncture can be a really efficient tool in having problem with the frequency and intensity of headaches. In a lot of clients Acupuncture can snuff out headaches entirely.

Acupuncture Helps Clients Battle Anxiety
Tons of clients struggling with anxiety, whether moderate, or extreme, are going through acupuncture as an accessory treatment for their condition in the last few years.

Acupuncture Assists With Weight-loss
Acupuncture can reinforce a client's durability, assistance battle yearnings, and improve a client's capability to react favorably to healthy diet plan and workout choices.

Advantages of Acupressure and Acupuncture in Asthma Sufferers
Needle acupuncture has revealed symptomatic relief to people with asthma in some research studies. As an alternative technique of promoting acupuncture points, acupressure might also have the prospective to supply comparable advantages to asthma victims.

Tension Management:
Acupuncture has been a tested technique for tension relief, and as we lower our tension level a lot of other illness will vanish. That is since an acupuncturist is dealing with the root of the issue and not the signs only.

Acupuncture for Strong pain Management:
Everyone experiences some real pain or pain throughout their life time. Acupuncture will help to enhance severe and persistent real pain issues. Acupuncture promotes the brain to launch chemicals (hormonal agents) that act a lot like natural opiates. Acupuncture can promote the brain to produce endorphin release, (an endorphin is a natural real pain relief compound that make us feel great) so after treatment you will feel more calm and relaxed.

Cosmetic/ Face Lift Impact:
In current years, there is a ton of discuss making use of acupuncture for facial restoration that acupuncture promotes. There are a lot of methods to enhance your appearance and acupuncture is just one of the best and simplest methods to look 5 to ten years more youthful. It is very important to bear in mind that so as to accomplish these actual results you will really need at least 10 treatments and continuing care by your acupuncturist.

Acupuncture and Weight Reduction:
It is clear that acupuncture will not make you slim down but it can help you on your course. Some of the primary reasons that we are unable to stay with any diet plan are as it is tough to manage yearnings, keep one's cool and change your way of life.
This is where acupuncture begins to work. It is popular that acupuncture will help to manage yearnings, lower cravings and alleviate tension. Psychological eaters will considerably take advantage of this. As a result, way of life changes are going to be much easier with less bumps in the roadway to health.

Acupuncture to Quit Smoking Cigarettes:
Lots of people do not know that acupuncture is a great tool to help you keep away from cigarettes. Needles will not make you quit, but they will help you remain on track. Acupuncture will help by minimizing withdrawal signs. These signs are (not restricted to): tension, stress and anxiety, sleeping disorders, uneasyness, and psychological distress. Acupuncture is an alternative to make these signs much easier and more manageable. For that reason, the very first choice you make to quit smoking is to try to find an acupuncturist who can begin you on the roadway to health.

Acupuncture reduces Migraines
Acupuncture has been shown to stop migraines. The technique used to deal with migraines is to get rid of the origin of the migraine, and that is stress. Another advantage of acupuncture treatment to a migraine patient is that it is pain-free, and there are also no negative effects of the process.

Acupuncture Decreases Diabetes Manifestations
If you are searching for methods to naturally manage your diabetes signs, you might think about acupuncture as a practical form of treatment.

Acupuncture is primarily pain-free, but often a small puncturing feeling might be felt when needles are placed. Continued research on the impacts and advantages of the acupuncture program that this technique can be an efficient main treatment in health care along with a helpful adjunctive treatment. Among its enticing functions is no adverse effects when carried out by a certified acupuncturist.

How Acupuncture Actually Functions

You may be asking why the Chinese pierce needles in their skin. You may presume that those are things for a circus or a masochist to practice. Actually, the process is called acupuncture, the poking of needles into the skin is a recovery art, a medical treatment that truly works.

Acupuncture is connected with Standard Chinese Medication (TCM) for a truth that acupuncture has its roots in age-old China.

How Acupuncture Functions

Boring great filiform needles into certain points in the body is a method used for acupuncture to reduce strong pain or for restorative functions. These points, according to TCM, lie where the qi or the life energy streams. Meridian is the term used for parts of energy flow.

It is in the 12 primary meridians where most acupuncture points exist, which compare the essential body organs like the kidney, liver, and lungs. There are numerous disorders can be dealt with through acupuncture. Popular in the West are the acupuncture for the treatment of uncomfortable conditions like arthritis and headache along with acupuncture for weight-loss treatment.

This age-old Chinese recovery art was bombarded with many criticisms from researchers and Western physicians arguing that there is no physiological or histological basis for acupuncture points.

However in some way research studies show that acupuncture works for some conditions in spite of being thought about by some as quackery. In the 20th century, an extensive clinical research was performed but still acupuncture was not well comprehended when it concerns its efficiency.

A balance between yin and yang in the body requires health in TCM. These are opposing forces that interact in synergy. Yin and yang can be compared to dark and light, male and female, or low and high. Womanhood is associated to yin while masculinity is for yang.

The totally free flow of blood and qi are the most essential elements of TCM in acupuncture. Since qi has no comparable term in English, it is barely translated but more or less, it can be thought about as a type of life energy.

In certain parts of the body, qi is in some cases extreme or lacking and sometimes qi in the body has stagnancy. Draining pipes the excess of qi, promoting its completely free flow, and renewing it if there is a shortage are the goals of acupuncture.

To cover all of it, the recovery art of acupuncture is exceptional. Its efficiency in the treatment of different conditions can't be denied even for researchers no matter being declared by some as quackery.

If you are experiencing a specific disorder, you can think about acupuncture for a 100% natural and safe treatment. For centuries, acupuncture has been practiced for great reason.

Some Myths about Acupuncture

Although the practice of acupuncture has been around for countless years, it is still the topic of tons of myths. Acupuncture is just one of the fastest growing fields of natural medicine, and is even covered by a lot of medical insurance and state worker's payment strategies. Here are 8 of the largest myths.

No Scientific Basis
Acupuncture might be a kind of natural medicine, but peer evaluated research studies have found that acupuncture treatments do associate to a decrease in the client's viewed levels of real pain.

Needles Not Safe
This myth associates with the misconception that the needles used in acupuncture treatments can carry illness or are unhygienic. Acupuncture needles can be found in sanitized, sealed, bundles. The needles are only used. After usage in treatment the needles are dealt with as medical waste and effectively gotten rid of. You have as much to fear from an unclean needle at the acupuncturist as you do at the physician for the needle used in a shot. Acupuncture Treatments are Needed Daily to Work

Acupuncture hurts
Usually, acupuncture is almost pain-free. Some clients report feeling a small pinch, less than common with a chance at the physician, with the application of an acupuncture needle. Acupuncture works, in part, to unwind the body and bring back balance. Triggering real pain is not an efficient technique for acupuncture treatment.

Acupuncture and Standard Chinese Medication are the exact same
Acupuncture uses the concepts and comprehension of standard Chinese medication, though it is its own independent discipline. Conventional Chinese medication also counts on natural solutions Tai-Qi.

Acupuncture Sessions Last a Long Period Of Time
A normal acupuncture session lasts half an hour to one hour. This consists of the pre acupuncture assessment and the time it requires to make a medical diagnosis and develop a treatment strategy.

Acupuncture needs to be done every day to Work
Every client is different. Nevertheless, many clients do not really need everyday treatment. A lot of clients really need to get a series of acupuncture treatments, but the sessions are generally once a week to once a month. Clients that really need day-to-day sessions are unusual and usually the everyday sessions are only for a quick amount of time till the intense issue is brought under control.

The Needles are long

Acupuncture needles been available in a range of sizes. The majority of acupuncture needles are less than a half of an inch in length. A common hypodermic needle is about the exact same length as an acupuncture needle, but is also much thicker.

Anybody can be an Acupuncturist
The large bulk of states need a strenuous licensing process for acupuncturist. A licensed acupuncturist must finish 4 years obviously deal with a scientific internship of over 1,000 hours. Furthermore, right before getting an acupuncturist license, candidates should pass an evaluation. Lots of acupuncturists also initially acquire a university degree. Once certified, to keep their license in great standing, acupuncturist need to go to routine continuing education classes and follow the security and ethical requirements of their occupation. Acupuncturists become part of the healthcare community.

Natural Medicine in General

Most current research found programs that acupuncture treatments are more effective in dealing with many medical conditions. The expenses of acupuncture treatments can cost numerous dollars to as much as countless dollars which truly depends upon the quality of treatments and the length of acupuncture treatments needed. In addition, there are a ton of acupuncture treatments that goes farther than placing a needle. More research has recorded findings that it's not totally understood how acupuncture approaches works totally, though there are some points that acupuncture enhances the production of endorphins that makes the whole body feel entirely relaxed and help in reducing tension.

Acupuncture treatments have recorded to be great success in dealing with injuries connected to tense, scarred or inflamed tendons, stress or muscles. It has also been found that people do not know that acupuncture treatments are great treatments for anxiety, allergic reactions, tension, stress and anxiety, sleeping disorders and sinus problems. It is found that recently more people are checking out acupuncture treatment for weight-loss.

Some proof show that acupuncture treatments are really efficient than non-active medications for alleviating post-treatment real pain and is kept at follow-up. Acupuncture treatments take around 25 minutes, but again the acupuncture treatment can differ, depending upon the client's condition. Many acupuncture treatments can also be offered at the same time with other medical treatments, just like standard Western medication, chiropractic changes and or naturopathic prescriptions. Nevertheless, it is rather general with the very first number of acupuncture treatments to have some experience of great relaxation and also some moderate incomprehension straight following the treatment.

Acupuncture treatment includes a series of weekly or biweekly treatments in an outpatient setting. It appears that acupuncture treatment is extremely beneficial as a private treatment for some health conditions, but acupuncture also much more used in mix with other standard Western medical treatments. A lot of research studies have found that acupuncture treatment can minimize the number of Reynaud's phenomenon; helps enhance conditions like irritable bowel syndrome; together with improve other medical treatments for gout, if used with combined treatment.

There is a frustrating bulk of clients who find that acupuncture treatments are rather comfortable and extremely relaxing. Many clients actually drop off to sleep throughout treatment although it is a fast process. An acupuncture technique applies heat, needles, pressure and other acupuncture treatments to many areas on the skin called acupuncture points. Right before starting acupuncture treatment, ask the acupuncturist chosen about the amount of treatments suggested and an approximated expense of the treatments.

Acupuncture treatments are ending up being more accepted by the public and by doctors. The majority of acupuncture treatment is also practiced by certain licensed doctors that come from some expert Acupuncture companies that release semi-annual journals. The acupuncture treatments have worked in a range of parts in the healthcare field. In more research, research studies on acupuncture treatment will not be only significant for the health and well-being of the client but also essential for the improvement of medical science. Significant debate has surrounded acupuncture; on the one hand, big claims have been produced for its performance, on the other hand, acupuncture has been critiqued for its lack of clinical standing.

Acupuncture is a Chinese medical treatment which includes the activation of bottom lines in your body using diligently placed needles and it needs different kinds of acupuncture devices. With the growing need for acupuncture treatments, these acupuncture supplies and devices are easily supplied to the marketplace to guarantee that your client gets the most satisfying acupuncture treatment attainable.

Conventional Chinese medication centers have big variations as far as the used acupuncture supplies are concerned. Often contamination controls are carried out to check the conventional Chinese medication items so as to preserve an acupuncture medical center safe.

Needles

The acupuncture needle is absolutely the standard and most crucial acupuncture instrument. It has the capability to produce impressive recovery actual results. Comprehending how acupuncture needles are produced, the numerous kinds of manages, used metals and needle ideas will enable you to pick the right needle for the appropriate application on the client. Despite the fact that tons of acupuncture items do not penetrate the skin like e.g. acupuncture needles, tidiness is still a considerable matter.

A lot of specialist acupuncturists use pre-sterilized needle plans planned to be gotten rid of after the treatment of each client. Acupuncture needles are readily available in certain sizes and sizes, depending upon their intent and on which part of the body they are to be used. In age-old Chinese process, there have been as much as 9 types of needles. Needles are crafted from certain metals just like gold and silver, in addition to much less basic products comparable to stone or bones. In modern acupuncture, the most normal form of needle is the metal filiform, or thread-like needle made from stainless-steel.

Moxa Sticks

Many specialists of acupuncture also perform moxibustion and need to source moxa items amongst their other acupuncture supplies. It is a kind of heat treatment which promotes acupuncture points on the body. Because of that, acupuncture supplies usually consist of organic items for moxibustion, moxa sticks or rolls, incense and extinguishers for moxibustion. Normally, the moxa wool is compressed or rolled into a stogie shape, and this makes it easy for the professional to guide the burning coal over the body. A really essential variation of the typical moxa stick includes smokeless moxa, which is generally a carbonized mix of moxa and herbs. This makes it virtually smokeless when burned. Sook moxa sticks are made from a mix of wormwood, sagebrush and mugwort which produce a great scent of burning wood.

A Cupping Set

The cupping treatment therapy is an alternative treatment by which cups are located onto the skin to produce suction. The cups are made from different products, that include earthenware, glass and bamboo. Supporters of cupping treatment really believe that the suction of the cups sets in motion blood flow to boost the recuperating of a vast array of health issues. Nowadays, there are certain cupping sets readily available on the marketplace which incorporate the use of magnets and an air pump often in mix with a hot flame.

Models and Charts
Acupuncture models are usually used by expert acupuncturists. A lot of acupuncture supply shops save these auxiliary items. These acupuncture models are a specific reproduction of the body which suggests the acupuncture points on the meridians, which typically works as guides to find these points on a genuine client. These models are usually constructed out of resilient soft vinyl plastic product and installed on a strong wood platform.

Security and Dangers

To tons of the Chinese professionals of acupuncture, who are highly trained and committed to helping an entire series of conditions with their abilities, it must appear strange that beyond China acupuncture security and threats would be a problem.

Acupuncture has been practiced for more than 2,000 years in China and yet, weird as it might appear, it has only in the last twenty years become popular outside the East.

Acupuncture security and threats are still a problem however, as acupuncture remains an approach of treatment which is thought about unverified by the medical occupation.

The existing main view is that the jury is still out on whether acupuncture actually does work. This holds true though a great deal of reports on it, both in United States and in other places, has been finished.

Research studies have included big research studies on the strategy performed in China. But, regardless of that the medical occupation still thinks about the jury to be out on whether acupuncture has considerable advantageous results.

If it was clear that there were huge advantages, as might yet still be shown, acupuncture security and threats would be stabilized against the apparent enhancements offered. If the advantages were clinically shown to be big it would be a simple matter to show that it was beneficial for people to take the treatment, even acknowledging some acupuncture threats exist.

The point being made by some leading authorities on natural medicines is that till the capability of acupuncture is medically shown to minimize strong pain, practically any threat from the process is way too much threat, and for this reason the process ends up being inadvisable as a matter of concept.

This is a really difficult test to use, and one would ask whether, if a client had the ability to stay away from taking proposed painkiller just like aspirin. Paracetamol and codeine after acupuncture that would not in itself validate the treatment? Even these drugs, which we take without more idea, do come with threats to our health, though at a really low level.

No medical professionals seem recommending that the threat of an unfavorable experience with acupuncture is anything aside from really low when the treatments are performed by well trained specialists. In simple fact, right across certain research studies now finished with great deals of people in the study hall acupuncture security is not actually an issue in the large bulk of cases, and for that reason dangers seem extremely low.

Several deaths have happened within a big sample in a Chinese research study, but info is reported as being scanty on the situations of death, and might people might conclude that the extremely little portion of deaths could quickly be represented without associating substantial threat to the treatment. The different other research studies show that when practiced by highly qualified specialists in acupuncture the primary threats seem about health and the sanitation of the needless used.

Medical mistakes might take place when needling too deeply, or in the really wrong fishing of needling insertion. Some issue cases have been related to needling for pain in the back reduction, if the needle is not positioned properly,

In some cases there has been specialist mistake and/or neglect, but that happens in all walks of life at a really low frequency, and acupuncture is not likely to be any different.

For people thinking about acupuncture treatment we suggest that your remember the existing medical occupation's main view that the method is unverified for the decrease of strong pain till research studies show otherwise.

It is also possible that if you do not get medical guidance on your grievance, right before getting acupuncture treatment, an underlying cause might not be detected, so always get medical guidance first.

The choice must be yours, and the threat which you choose is beneficial should be stabilized by the advantages which you view you will get from the treatment. You really need to weigh up the balance of advantage against threat for yourself. It is your choice.

Different Acupuncture Designs

If you do not know much about acupuncture, it can be puzzling to learn that there are different designs or schools, with different approaches and methods of practicing. This post clarifies the primary distinctions, to help you choose what is right for you.

Medical or Conventional?
The primary distinction is between the modern-day, Western methods of working (so called 'medical acupuncture') and the old, asian designs (' standard acupuncture'.) These 2 are so different, that to call them both by the name 'acupuncture' is rather deceptive.

Medical Acupuncture is a current creation, based completely on the concepts of Western clinical medication. Training courses for certified Western professionals (such as GPs, nurses, physios etc) are extremely brief - generally around 5 days. This treatment is used nearly specifically for real pain relief, though it might sometimes be used for other conditions. In some cases physiotherapists just like chiropractic specialists or physios use this type of acupuncture in their practice, in which case it is often called 'dry needling'.

Conventional Acupuncture is the age-old treatment developed in China, and now extensively practiced right across South East Asia and the world. It is a holistic treatment, based upon an importantly different way of seeing health and illness. Training courses take around 3 years. It is most likely 'conventional' acupuncture that you come up with when you come up with acupuncture. It can be used a really vast array of physical, psychological and psychological conditions.

Kinds Of Conventional Acupuncture
The primary style of conventional acupuncture practiced all over the world is TCM (' Conventional Chinese Medication'.) This is what is taught and practiced in China, and is the requirement for many Western courses in conventional acupuncture. It has a history extending back over 2000 years, and given the name TCM in the 1950s when a structured curriculum was very first created for mentor right across China (till then there were lots of local variations).

Other nations have developed somewhat different designs of their own, for example Japanese acupuncture which is understood for its really mild strategies, and usage of abdominal area medical diagnosis (feeling the abdominal area as a diagnostic tool). Korean acupuncture also has a little different theories, and it tends to prefer dealing with constitutional issues. Some Korean acupuncturists only use acupuncture points on the hands for their treatments. On the entire however, Japanese and Korean acupuncture are rather comparable to TCM.

Auricular acupuncture uses acupuncture points on the ears to deal with health problem. It can be used along with other designs (in which case body points will also be used) or by itself. A current creation - the NADA procedure - uses 5 acupuncture points on the ear in the treatment of dependency.

5-elements acupuncture was created in the 1950s by an Englishman, JR Worsley, who had trained in different nations in Asia. It concentrates on dealing with constitutional imbalances, and is said to concentrate on mental and psychological conditions (though these can also be dealt with by other designs of standard acupuncture). It is rather different in theory and practice to TCM.

Finally, 'Classical Acupuncture' is a brand-new term for an old medication. It is a catch all term to define age-old methods of practicing that precede TCM, especially including Taoist ideas and strategies.

Selecting an acupuncturist.
It is important that you know the distinction between medical and conventional acupuncture, but the distinctions between different standard designs may well not issue you much.
If you are searching for an acupuncturist, more vital things to think about are the professionals training and experience. Just how long have they been in practice, and have they treated your condition right before? Do they practice any other branches of Chinese medication that could also serve to you? (Tuina massage, herbs, qi gong, nutrition.) And most importantly, do you proceed with them and trust them?
WHT I MDIL ACUPUNCTURE?

Acupuncture is an older Chinese medical art. It is a method of placing and controlling great needles into particular points on the body with the aim of easing strong pain and for healing purpose. There are lots of techniques to learning and practicing it. Medical acupuncture is the term used to define acupuncture carried out by a physician trained and accredited in Western medication that has also had through training in acupuncture as a specialized practice. Such a physician or health expert might use one or the other technique, or a mix of both, to deal with a dysfunction or disease.

How Medical acupuncture Progressed.
Research study of standard Chinese Medication takes great deal of time. That is the reason Medical acupuncture was created for western specialists who wants to use the methods of acupuncture together with other medical technique. Medical acupuncture was created for medical physicians, physio therapists, chiropractics physician and osteopaths. The person when find out about acupuncture is referred to as acupuncturists. The term natural medicine is typically used in the modern-day western world includes any recovery practice that doesn't fall within the world of traditional medication. Acupuncture is thought about to be among such alternative medical method. Medical acupuncture is an effort by evidence-based medication to comprehend the results of acupuncture from a western, clinical perspectives instead of within the paradigm of Chinese standard medication.

How Medical acupuncture different from Classical acupuncture.
Medical acupuncture is a modern form of acupuncture that was developed by Medical professionals in the western world. In medical acupuncture the standard theory of points and meridians is either disregarded completely or is significantly reinterpreted since there is allegedly no physically proven physiological or histological basis for the presence of acupuncture points or meridians. Also in case of medical acupuncture the principles of illness are stemmed from contemporary western pathology rather than Chinese medical theory which precedes usage of the clinical approach. Last but not least the medical acupuncture is comprehended to work by means of the western biomedical understanding.

World Health Company (W.H.O.) suggestion.
Following are the conditions for which Acupuncture is advised by W.H.O.
Breathing Illnesses like intense sinus problems, severe rhinitis, acute rhinitis, severe tonsillitis.

Bronchopulmonary Illnesses just like severe bronchitis, bronchial asthma.

Eye Disorders like severe conjunctivitis, cataract (without problems), myopia, main retinitis.

Conditions of the mouth cavity just like tooth pain, real pain after tooth extraction, gingivitis, pharyngitis.

Orthopedic Conditions like periathritis humeroscapularis, tennis elbow, sciatica, low neck and back pain, rheumatoid arthritis.

Food poisonings just like convulsion of the esophagus and cardia, missteps, gastrophosis, severe and persistent gastritis, stomach hyperacidity, persistent duodenal ulcer, severe and persistent colitis, severe bacterial dysentery, diarrhea, paralytic ileus.

Neurological Conditions like headache, migraine, trigeminal neuralgia, facial paralysis, paralysis after apoplectic fit, peripheral neuropathy, paralysis brought on by poliomyelitis, meniere's syndrome, neurogenic bladder dysfunction, nighttime enuresis, intercostals neuralgia.

Modern clarification.
There are 2 efforts at western medical clarification about the system of acupuncture.
The big gate theory of strong pain by Patrick Wall and Robert Melzack which postulates the presence of gates or filters in the spine that can regulate transference of real pain info within the nerve system.

The 2nd clarification is based upon the presence of natural opiatus in the main nerve system and in other places in the body. It is the strong pain eliminating compounds like endorphins and encephalin.

The Points Chart

Acupuncture returns a long way and it is all fixated the basis of certain points within the body. You should know what these points are and where they lie for acupuncture to help you. If you really need to know the positioning of the acupuncture points then you really need a chart and you really need to know how to read it effectively? An acupuncture chart is a great way for a brand-new therapist to find out about the points and where they lie and it's also helpful for somebody who will be getting acupuncture and just would like to know how it works.

Acupuncture is an old form of medication in which certain points on the body are used as treatment for other issues or discomforts within the body. There are actually numerous points on the body, situated on different meridians from head to toe. It can be hard to keep up with all of them and an acupuncture point's chart can help you do this. You should never ever try to perform acupuncture on yourself when you aren't certified to do so but lots of people just take pleasure in understanding where the certain points are and how they work so they can better comprehend their treatment.

But there is more to learn a lot from an acupuncture point's chart than just what the certain points are. You can also find out about where they lie on the body along with the command points, the Prominent points, the 4 seas points and more. These are generally written in a letter-number mix abbreviation that once you become more knowledgeable about reading and blogging about the acupuncture charts, you will remember what they represent.

In addition, this chart can also teach you areas, descriptions, functions and also the scientific applications for the acupuncture points. You can discover the cun, which are measurements used to find the points on a specific person's body. If you want to find out more about acupuncture points, how to find them for yourself, what they do and more, you really need an acupuncture point's chart.

Whether you are brand-new to acupuncture, thinking about getting it yourself as a treatment or just somebody studying and would like to know more about it, you can benefit considerably from an acupuncture points chart.

Possible Negative Effects
The needles used in the treatment procedure of acupuncture are revealed to produce unexpected leaks in the lungs. This could be serious since it triggers partial collapse of the lungs. The contagious adverse effects consist of liver disease and some bacterial infections in the sites of needle insertion. These negative effects can be gotten rid of if the person doing the acupuncture takes correct preventive steps.

More about Points

" What are acupuncture points? Do they have something to do with nerves?" In simple fact, acupuncture points truly do not have much to do with nerves at all. What they are, and how they have the ability to impact all sorts of elements of health is a little a mind-bending trip. Are you prepared to take the red tablet?

A lot more than Real pain Management
If you take a look around in the media you'll ultimately discover somebody describing that acupuncture is just an adjustment of nerves that leads to the body launching endorphins.

Endorphins are the feel-good chemicals of the brain. The endorphins, the hypothesis goes, and after that act to moderate the experience of real pain in the body. It's a neat, straight-forward answer that's simple for the majority of people to accept. It is also clearly woefully insufficient.

The issue with this hypothesis is that real pain is just one thing acupuncture can be used to deal with. Endorphins can't clarify how acupuncture can be used to control menstruations, improve fertility, aid sleeping disorders, open overloaded sinuses, deal with digestion problems, help people quit smoking and so on. Undoubtedly there needs to be more to acupuncture than the release of endorphins.

Caves
The word for "acupuncture point" in Chinese is "xué". The leading point of the character for this word is said to represent a covering while the bottom part represents a hole. The word is also translated as "cavern". So the word "point" is really missing some of the associations of the initial Chinese word.

An acupuncture point is a 3-dimensional thing. It is a cavern. It offers an access to something deep. What lies underneath the surface area is acupuncture channels. Acupuncture channels (often called "meridians") are a subject in and of themselves, but are beyond the scope of the post.

That said it suffices to comprehend that acupuncture points supply a deep access to the energy of the body.

Field Impacts
Through the last century or so the science of physics has started to brighten some of the odd guidelines by which deep space works. Energy and matter were found to be interchangeable. We started to see that matter exists as a wave or a field of unlimited size. Initially it was thought that quantum mechanics only applied to the extremely tiny world of atomic particles. Just recently research released in the clinical journal "Nature" has revealed that quantum impacts can be observed crazes huge enough to see with the naked eye.

The structure of "modern-day science" is Greek viewpoint. The structure for the science of acupuncture is Chinese Taoist viewpoint. Increasingly more these 2 sciences define deep space in comparable terms. I see this as a sign of development, as they both effort to define deep space as it actually exists.

Acupuncture works on the natural field of the body. Like a pebble dropped into a still pond, needles placed into acupuncture points send out ripples out as they get in and communicate with the energetic field of the body.

Each point has several particular results on some element of the body. Some act mostly in the location of the body close to the point. Others can have results on the far side of the body. Still other ones have an organized impact on the body. Using the science of Chinese medication an acupuncturist understands which indicates choose to attain a specific impact on the body that will bring it back to a state of health.

Found, Not Created
As humans, acupuncture points belong of our energetic anatomy. They have always existed. Through mindful observation and experimentation over countless years the acupuncture points were gradually found.

Taoist approach permitted the age-old Chinese to develop an comprehension of the laws of nature and the universes. It was through this grasp of the guidelines of deep space that the system of acupuncture had the ability to be found and deciphered.

You might have an interest in more concrete specifics about how acupuncture is used in particular health conditions. For example, you can read about acupuncture for menstruation policy along with acupuncture for sleep conditions at these links.

Acupuncture for Pain In The Back

Acupuncture is a standard medical practice that came from the Far East 2 thousand years ago. Due to its tested recovery capability, acupuncture is getting acknowledgment in the west. The medical market is gradually acknowledging this conventional recovery technique which is popular in recovery neck and back pain.

To be talked about below are 3 kinds of acupuncture approaches that help in minimizing or recovering neck and back pain.

The Chinese, Standard Way
Chinese standard acupuncture opened up the door for acupuncture's intro worldwide phase. It is thought about as the most well-known kind of acupuncture approach. Acupuncture has been used and is still being used in China to treat a range of different disease, among which is pain in the back. Needles are used in this kind of acupuncture which aims to manage or stabilize the flow of qi in your body. A well balanced qi flow will help a client alleviate his neck and back pain.

The Japanese, Conventional Way
This acupuncture technique resembles the Chinese technique but it uses needles which are thinner than the ones used in the latter. The use of needles in this type makes the technique moreover of the Chinese. This technique also aims to manage and stabilize the flow of qi in the body.

The Korean, Standard Way

Another kind of acupuncture for recovery pain in the back is the Korean conventional acupuncture. Compared to the very first 2 approaches, the Korean kind of acupuncture is more current but it is as reliable in recovery pain in the back. In this technique, the needles are placed in the hands only and not on different parts of the body which is being done in the Chinese and Japanese types. The needles used are much littler and thinner.

Now that you know the most well-known kind of acupuncture approaches that can be used to ease or alleviate pain in the back, please keep in mind to consult your physician initially right before trying among these techniques. Your medical professionals could supply you medical info which can be used by acupuncture specialists as guide in the recovery treatment.

Staying healthy needs practices in avoidance, self-awareness and self-care. Understanding the underlying concepts of care and the health advantages that Standard Chinese Medication and acupuncture can use is one step closer to optimum health.

The healing advantages of acupuncture are typically misinterpreted. Following through on an appropriate course of acupuncture treatment could be the different between finding relief and continuing to deal with a persistent health condition.

Health is about great blood circulation. A typical condition that is usually dealt with effectively with Standard Chinese Medication (TCM) is Qi and Blood Stagnancy. Qi is acknowledged in TCM as a type of bioelectricity that distributes with blood through the body. Strong pain is blockage to qi and blood flow stopping the transport of recovery representatives found in blood and qi to the afflicted location.

Think of how the heart pumps blood through the whole body and you will comprehend how simple it can be to develop Qi and Blood Stagnancy. Blood is drained of the heart into big capillary called arteries. Blood is moved relatively quickly through these arteries with substantial pressure as heart muscles agreement. Arteries continue to narrow into really small vessels called blood vessels than ultimate spill the blood out into the narrow space between the body cells called interstitial space.

High blood pressure at this moment is weak. Body cells can draw out nutrients from blood cells that are speeding by so this is natural but the potential for blockage is great. Injury can harm and block blood circulation but easy muscle stress, poor posture, and artery blocking meals are some examples that can also restrain flow. Squeeze your hand and your knuckles turn white obstructing the flow of blood. If you tried to keep a tight fist for too long you would quickly start to feel tingling and tingling and ultimately real pain - Qi and Blood Stagnancy.

Persistent strong pain results when recovering representatives in the blood and qi cannot reach to fix the hurt location. Acupuncture treatment can help promote blood circulation and bring back the body's natural recovery capabilities. Acupuncture is a treatment suggesting it usually needs several treatments to fix an imbalance and bring back consistency in health. There are stages of treatment that are necessary to comprehend to appropriately use acupuncture as a reliable treatment for the relief of health problems just like persistent strong pain.

3 Stages of Acupuncture Treatment

Relief Treatment
Relief of symptomatic real pain/ imbalance
Regular treatments

Stabilization Treatment
Support relief treatment so signs do not return
Frequency is less

Upkeep Treatment
Keep stabilization treatment
Regular treatments aren't needed and only periodic

A brand-new acupuncture client will typically ask how many treatments it will require to solve their issue. There is no specific answer. Treatment strategies are distinct to each client and their particular imbalances. Actual results and length of treatment will differ according to seriousness of condition and the health of the client. For instance, a persistent condition might really need long term care in contrast to an intense condition. A client with a weak constitution might really need more treatment than a client with a strong constitution.

Acupuncture needles are really thin, disinfected, and strong rather than hollow. No compounds are injected into the client throughout an acupuncture treatment. Such injections generally develop remarkable changes that aren't naturally produced by the body. For instance, cortisone injections are typically used in Western medication for persistent strong pain. You can only get several shots a year as overuse can stop the body from producing its own cortisone naturally.

Regular acupuncture treatments are needed to awaken the body's own natural recovery capabilities and produce an accumulative and more advantageous impact. The healing gains of treatment build momentum from one treatment to the next. In a condition just like persistent strong pain - blood circulation is blocked stopping the recovery representatives found in blood to be provided. Acupuncture treatment can enhance blood circulation and in time eliminate real pain. An appropriate course of treatment that is usually accepted to be adequate to produce an advantageous influence is about 10 - 12 treatment sessions. A client stopping treatment after a number of sessions has not given their body the chance to experience the accumulative advantages of acupuncture treatment.

Relief treatment might need 2 to 3 treatments weekly for some weeks to relief a bulk of the real pain and bring back function. Once advantages are experienced after relief treatment it would be prematurely to stop treatment. Oftentimes recovery is not complete and to stop the repeating real pain stabilization treatment is required. Frequency of treatment might be 1 time each week or 1 treatment every other week. After observing stability in the condition through treatment then a client advances into upkeep care, which could be 1 treatment each month or every couple of months.

Acupuncture treatment is concentrated on promoting and preserving health instead of the needed but identifying care of Western medication, which primarily concentrates on injuries. An internship for a medical physician is usually done in an appearncy clinic - an injury focused environment.

Upkeep treatment is just something that is motivated under the scope of acupuncture and TCM. It only makes a lot of sense to be participated in avoidance to promote optimum Health through such treatments as acupuncture, organic medication, diet plan treatment, healthy way of life cycles, and workout like Tai Chi, Qigong, and meditation. Understanding how to look after yourself is power through knowledge. Teaching self-care is a basic part of acupuncture as a natural and holistic treatment for the mind, body and spirit. Avoidance begins with awareness of yourself and your individual imbalances and after that taking steps to bring back and keep optimum health.

Acupuncture Diet Plans for Better Treatment

Now that you have begun using acupuncture as an alternative treatment to your illness, it is extremely necessary that you support your healing with a well balanced acupuncture diet plan. You should also know that taking the right diet plan is what will make your treatment effective. For that reason you need to know what kinds of diet plan to adopt if you really want acupuncture to work for you.

Right before you actually choose an acupuncture diet plan to supplement your treatment, it is a good idea for you to see your medical professional. Your acupuncturist will tell you the diet plans you should take after your treatment. Be cautioned that picking an expert and certified acupuncturist is what you really need to know the right food to take. So, if you want to adapt to your brand-new diet plan, ensure your medical professional knows.

Today, organic diet plans have shown to be really efficient in handling health concerns. Some acupuncturists will advise you to take herbs or natural tea made from herbs. In addition, they might ask you to take natural tablets or supplements right before beginning an acupuncture treatment.

Whatever suggestions your medical professional will give, make sure to inform him or her of your allergic reactions to certain food or herbs. Doing this will help your acupuncturist offer you the best and proper diet plan for your acupuncture treatment.

When you take the right diet plan, the food helps to produce essential nutrients that can be extremely helpful in acupuncture. These nutrients make your body defense system to be more powerful and battle whatever is the reason for that condition in your body. This more makes acupuncture to be more efficient in your body by eliminating all the discomforts much faster. This procedure also makes more energy from acupuncture to connect to the impacted regions in your body.

For that reason, taking the right acupuncture diet plan is just one of the best methods you can make acupuncture treatment work for you. This is why you should know what to eat to match the effort of your acupuncturist on your health. You really need the right Diet plan for Your Acupuncture now if you should stay healthy at all times. So, find an expert acupuncturist to give you all the needed info on the right diet plan for your treatment. You can discover the right food for your acupuncture from the web as seen above.

Alzheimer's illness is a kind of dementia which impacts middle-aged and older people. It is a progressive illness that gradually kills the victim's afferent neuron in the brain. Alzheimer's is a rather intricate illness that appears to be triggered by some impacts. It is the most typical kind of dementia, representing approximately seventy percent of detected cases, and it understands no limits, being spread out right across different societies and impacting both males and women in equivalent procedure. Alzheimer's illness can be exceptionally difficult for the victim's family, who really typically find themselves remaining in the cutting edge when it pertains to supplying care and assistance. It should be kept in mind that the relative or members doing the caring will also really need a lot of assistance.

The care of an Alzheimer's client is rather a difficulty as the decrease is sluggish and unforeseeable and can advance at a much different speed. If it happens that Alzheimer's is identified, look for any regional services and help groups that are readily available from your medical professional's surgical treatment or inquire at your regional health center. There is not a single unique test for Alzheimer s, but usually the right medical diagnosis is accomplished by dismissing other reasons for amnesia, for instance: Parkinson's illness, small strokes, or anxiety. This illness typically raises its ugly head after the age of 60 or so, and the danger gets higher with age development. All the exact same, it must be kept in mind that Alzheimer's illness is not always a regular part of the aging procedure.

Alzheimer's can be referred to as the death of the mind right before the Body, and as such is a really challenging and dismal condition for any family to need to handle. Alzheimer's is reckoned to be a deadly illness, but the typical cause of death is typically another disease (like pneumonia) which can develop as a problem in a specific already badly damaged by Alzheimer's. The treatment of Alzheimer's Illness is still reasonably young, but scientists are extremely positive that the time is not too far when medications will appear that will have the ability to effectively deal with the signs of Azheimers.

What parts of the brain are impacted?
Alzheimer ultimately impacts most parts of the brain. Nevertheless, everyone is impacted in a different way as the illness advances. The primary brain areas impacted by Alzheimer are the frontal, temporal and the parietal lobes.

The frontal lobe lies at the front of the brain and manages a variety of functions just like intelligence, making choices, solving issues and other psychological and social functions. Damage to this location triggers decline in lifestyle and creates extreme issues for clients to look after themselves.

The temporal lobe lies at both temples and ears and they are accountable for the long and the short-term memories. Episodic memory helps us to bear in mind events just like where we parked our vehicle or where are our home secrets. Recalling such events needs the saving and obtaining procedures situated at our temporal lobe. The Capability to learn lies in these areas, so damage to these regions might result in amnesia. This loss triggers the failure to sign up brand-new info and obtain it later when needed.

Speech capability lies behind the temporal lobe at the parietal lobe. This area is also accountable for the visual system and allows visual analysis and stimuli. Damage to this location might trigger unusual speech and visual issues.

Alzheimer initially impacts the hippocampus which lies in the median temporal lobe of the brain. It is the location of the brain in which brand-new memories are formed. It then transfers to other parts impacting different functions like thinking or feelings. The cerebellum and the brain stem are the last regions of the brain to be impacted. This is when we lose control of standard functions just like breathing, heart-rate and high blood pressure. This is Alzheimer's last resulting in death.

What Happens to the Brain of an Alzheimer's Client?

What happens in the brain of Alzheimer's client to trigger all of the cognitive and behavioral signs of the illness? Alois Alzheimer was the very first to find the weird plaques and tangles; attributes of illness in the brain of among his client throughout an autopsy. For many years, Alzheimer's illness could only be detected with a high degree of precise post-mortem. Now scientists are discovering more about exactly what is going on in the brain of Alzheimer's client to trigger illness.

The brains of Alzheimer's client include neurofibrillary tangles inside nerve cells and clumps of fibers called aberrant plaques beyond nerve cells. These tangles and plaques, initially defined by Alois Alzheimer in 1907, are the primary reason for Alzheimer illness. Mental retardation takes place as a result of nerve cells being obstructed with tiny filaments, which are comprised of an unusual kind of Tau protein. Blocked nerve cells are no longer able to do their job and pass along the impulses they get from the environment. For that reason, handicapped nerve cells are one reason for cognitive disabilities connected with Alzheimer's illness. Mental retardation because of neurofibrillary tangles is also found in associated illness like Parkinson's illness.

Nevertheless, tangles and plaques aren't distinct for the development and development of Alzheimer. Research studies now suggest that dementia in Alzheimer's client is triggered by the shrinking and death of nerve cells and synaptic loss, not by tangles and plaques themselves. Nevertheless, according to a leading hypothesis, amyloid deposits play an early role by setting moving a waterfall of biochemical events that trigger the cells to diminish and die. Professionals also actually believe that reduced levels of the neurotransmitter acetylcholine, a chemical that bridges synapses between nerve cells that effect memory, also adds to amnesia of Alzheimer's illness.

Causes

The real reasons for Alzheimer's illness stay evasive. Nevertheless, scientists have made development in comprehending the neural roots of the incapacitating condition.

The illness is called after Alois Alzheimer, who was the very first to recognize the strange plaques and tangles in the brain, which is particular of the health problem. Till the last years of the twentieth century, Alzheimer's could be detected properly only by a post-mortem assessment.

Nowadays, researchers are starting to discover specifically what is going on and why those particular tangles and plaques turn up in the brain.

Lots of the signs of Alzheimer's illness are triggered by neurofibrillary tangles in the brain. Tiny filaments obstruct the nerve cells. These filaments are comprised of an irregular sort of Tau protein.

In a typical brain, Tau protein bonds into microtubules and makes it possible for transference of messages from one nerve cell to another. But in an Alzheimer brain, rather than bonding into message paths, Tau protein bonds with itself. And the nerve cell messages go absolutely nowhere.

Since the nerve cells are blocked, signals from the environment are no longer transferred the way they should be. That is why extreme cognitive disability is just one of the signs of Alzheimer's illness.

Researchers hypothesize that Tau protein breakdown which leads to neurofibrillary tangles is brought on by beta amyloid protein, but this is yet to be conclusively shown.

It is beta amyloid protein that triggers plaques between nerve cells, which is the other primary damage to the brain in Alzheimer's illness.

The plaque deposits are sticky spots in the brain which include beta amyloid protein. Plaque blocks communication paths between nerve cells, which leads to the memory issues and learning failures related to Alzheimer's illness.

The degree of cognitive disability depends upon the amount of plaque present. Plaque acts by hindering the typical performance of acetylcholine, which helps to send nerve messages.

Treatment for Alzheimer's illness includes using acetylcholinesterase inhibitors, which works by obstructing enzymes that take in the acetylcholine. This medication works throughout the early phases of the illness previously way too much plaque has already developed.

Some research appears to show that plaques trigger tangles. One research study took proteins from mice to remove the plaque-causing beta amyloid. They found that the proteins eliminated the tangles too. Comparable results have been caused by other medications too.

Others actually believe that both plaques and tangles are the outcome of other procedures. One possible offender is inflamed axons. Axons are vital for sending messages between nerve cells. When axons swell, they might block message transference and maybe cause the plaques and tangles which cause Alzheimer's illness.

Researchers are striving at discovering the reasons for Alzheimer's illness, which might eventually result in a thorough treatment for this feared condition.

Phases and Patterns

Alzheimer illness could be from moderate, moderate, reasonably extreme and extreme Alzheimer's illness or clarified as phases falling in general department of early-stage, mid-stage and late-stage classifications. Specialists have made a standard structure, mentioning the development of Alzheimer illness in its phase pattern of development. This structure is based

upon a system developed by Barry Reisberg, M.D., Scientific Director of the New York City University School of Medication's Silberstein Aging and Dementia Proving Ground.
The phase pattern development of Alzheimer illness provides for helpful referral for how the illness might unfold and therefore assisting the members of the family for future element. Though developing of the Alzheimer illness might or might not happen according to the structure, their development might not be at the exact same rate as people with Alzheimer illness die approximately 4 to 6 years after medical diagnosis. But Alzheimer illness can have period differing from 3 to even extending till twenty years right before eliminating the client.

Phase 1: No disability
The client will be typically operating like any other regular person. This person will experience no memory issues and therefore the Alzheimer illness will not appear to healthcare specialist.

Phase 2: Really Moderate Cognitive decrease
Essentially in this phase the person with Alzheimer illness will begin having the standard signs of really moderate cognitive decrease like forgetting of glasses, memory lapse or loss specifically of names or familiar word and places. But these signs will essentially be neglected or be called as typical age associated changes, whereas these are the early indications of Alzheimer illness. These signs again will not appear to doctor and even to family, good friends or co workers.

Phase 3: Moderate Cognitive decrease
This is the phase when people dealing with the impacted person acknowledge of him having some issue. This is the phase when Alzheimer illness can be identified, yet all people suffering aren't identified in this phase. In this phase, client experiences issues with memory and concentration.

Fundamental signs of the phase are:
Trouble in using word or names
Trouble in capability to keep in mind brand-new names of person introduced
Efficiency problems in social and work settings
Checking out trouble as passage is little kept.
Losing and losing important thing
Issue in preparation and organizing

Phase 4: Moderate cognitive decrease
A mindful assessment results in the verification of person being experiencing Alzheimer illness. This is the moderate phase of Alzheimer illness. As the client begins experiencing:

Forgetting current events or existing celebrations, sometimes they keep in mind and sometimes they forget.
Disability in psychological math
Trouble in doing complicated job
Minimized memory of individual history

Feeling of privacy and seclusion as impacted individual feel suppressed and withdrawn.

Phase 5: Moderate Extreme cognitive decrease
This is the worrying phase where essentially relatives should begin putting on more attention to the client. As the client begins struggling with significant spaces in memory and deficits in cognitive function. Support with daily activities is now important. Generally in this phase the person will:

Throughout a medical interview will be not able to remember essential specifics like present address, their phone number which therefore is worrying simple fact that not to leave them to roam alone.
State of confusion: they reveal a ton of confusion as why they are here, what were they doing and what date it is or perhaps matter of simple fact what season it is.
Required assistance selecting appropriate clothes for the season or the event
Difficulties with psychological math; therefore managing monetary activity could be pressure. Though at this phase, it is not as serious as they normally keep crucial knowledge about themselves like understanding their own name and the names of their partner or kids.
At this phase they do not need support with eating or using the toilet

Phase 6: Serious cognitive decrease
The phase when the individual requirements his family assistance to the optimum, as memory troubles get extreme and character of the person might even change and there is comprehensive requirement for care of the client as popular day-to-day activities also become an inconvenience for the client.
The person will have issues and signs like:

Lose most listening of current experiences and awareness of events in addition to of their environments
Recollection of their individual history is imperfect, though usually remember their own name
Sometimes forgetting the name of their partner, main caretaker though can usually differentiate familiar faces from unknown faces
Required assist with dressing appropriately as they might make mistakes like putting pajamas over daytime outfits, wearing winter season outfits in summer season or shoes on really wrong feet
Experience condition of their typical sleep/waking cycle
Required assistance even when going toileting, they might really need assist with flushing toilet, wiping and getting rid of tissue appropriately.
Have increasing episodes of urinary or fecal incontinence
Experience significant character changes and flaunting behavioral signs like suspiciousness and deceptions. For instance, they tend to really believe that their caretaker is an impostor, might even have hallucinations i.e. seeing or hearing things that aren't truly there; and even experience compulsive and repeated habits that can be hand-wringing or tissue shredding
Tend to go roaming and after that become lost not understanding how they came there.

Phase 7: Really serious cognitive decrease

This is the late phase of Alzheimer illness, the last in structure when the individual lose the majority of its capabilities and his muscles and nerves begins deteriorating and lose of weight is remarkable. This is the phase, where it is better to include a nurse or put them in healthcare center, as the people who are residing in with client will feel extremely miserable and their failure to help much will trigger them strong pain.

Person will:

Loose capability to react to environment

Loose Capability to speak: losing capability for identifiable speech though word or expressions might be said.

Loose Capability to manage movement and reflexes: need assist with even the fundamental activity like eating, and toileting. Loose capability to walk without help, as phase weakens; capability to sit without assistance will also go.

Loose smile: they will have no expression on their face, as they will unable to smile or perhaps maintain their head. Reflexes become unusual, swallowing impaired and muscles ending up being stiff.

The Impacts of the Condition

A meaning of the impacts of Alzheimer's illness would most likely be that it can begin with no real recognizable signs, and continues to gradually worsen gradually. The illness begins by impacting certain cells in our brain. Once Alzheimer's illness takes hold it slowly starts to harm the brain cells as much as the point where they ultimately die.

Signs will consist of the wear and tear of memory, impacts thinking capability, and the capability to hold regular proficient discussions. Tons of researchers are in contract with the principle that Alzheimer's illness begins to begin since the body begins to over produce a particular protein frequently called beta-amyloid protein. The extreme production of the specific protein leads to the brain cells being assaulted.

The Impacts of Alzheimer's illness become more typical in people once they have reached the age of seventy. It can in many cases impact people who are in their fifties, but the chances are that if an individual is over seventy, the chances of contracting the illness are increased greatly. It is thought that at least half of the people that enjoy their eighties experience some form of Alzheimer's illness. Among the significant reasons that Alzheimer's is on the boost in the western world is that people are living longer, so the more older the population is the more people will struggle with the illness.

Simply because you are aging, it does not mean that you will absolutely catch the illness. There are a lot of people who have reached a high number of years, and have never ever had an issue with Alzheimer's. It is also thought that another impact of Alzheimer's illness is that specific kinds of genes are more vulnerable to get Alzheimer's illness. That means if somebody has struggled with the illness, then the chances of their progeny developing that illness will be much higher.

There are certain other reasons that might begin the start of Alzheimer's illness. Things like high blood pressure, diabetes, higher levels of cholesterol, and heart problem, and consistent tension, can all contribute to Alzheimer's. On the other hand there are people who have experienced the conditions above and gone on to live lives totally without the illness. The truth of the matter is that we cannot determine the precise reasons for Alzheimer's, and at the moment it is primarily uncertainty based upon the research done so far.

The primary issue is that the number of people who experience Alzheimer's is growing and we do not know why. The repercussions of the illness can be exceptionally serious, not only on the people who experience it but on the people who need to take care of, and watch the patients going through the procedure. All of us really need to become conscious of what sort of indications to try to find. This is actually crucial as medication can be provided for the patients of Alzheimer's illness, which will help decrease the impacts of Alzheimer's illness, and the damage of the brain cells.

Signs of Alzheimer s

Clinically speaking, our brain has following practical departments:
(1) The biggest part is, as they call, the Cerebrum,
(2) the Cerebellum, and.
(3) the Brain Stem.

They interact to support all your psychological and exercises, anything you do intentionally and unwittingly: from the time you wake to the time you fall in the sleep and also throughout the duration of sleep. To put it simply it is the brain that makes every little thing in your life possible.

The illness of Alzheimer doesn't spare any location of the brain untouched; it slowly attacks and impacts all regions of brain in the people experiencing this illness. As the illness keeps impacting numerous parts of the brain of the patient, brand-new signs continue emerging and this continues till the death of the person.

The following is the list of signs or psychological and handicaps manifesting in those struggling with this illness:

1. Issue of current amnesia.
2. Issue of Attention.
3. Issue of Language.
4. Issue in generation of speech.
5. Issue in social conduct.
6. Issue in feeling.
7. Issue of movement of body part.
8. Issue in determining of body parts.
9. Issue of self recognition.
10. Issue of unawareness of space/locality/ time.
11. Issue of sleep.
12. Issue of writing.
13. Issue of visual attention.
14. Issue of recognizing item.
15. Issue of reading.

16. Issue of hearing.
17. Issue of irritation/ anger.
18. Issue in acknowledgment of face.
19. Issue of long term memory.
20. Issue of sense of odor.
21. Issue of control on feeling.
22. Issue of current amnesia.
23. Coordination of great movement.
24. Issue in holding items.
25. Issue in making quick movement.

The Earliest Signs.

1. Amnesia:
The lapse of memory - specified as the forgetting the most current occurrences and the learned info. It advances in forgetting the most essential past dates, events, and even the names. In addition to it, prompting for any particular info again and again and depending on certain help to help one' self out (like pointer notes etc) or other members of the family for those things which were dealt with all by one's own self right before. But what is thought about regular is to forget names and visits on periodic basis.

2. Trouble in job efficiency.
People at an early phase of AD find trouble in preparation and performing the day-to-day jobs which were even familiar to them. To be more particular, people might forget the steps associated with preparing a meat, playing a game, or positioning a call and so on nevertheless it is regular to periodically forget what you were to do/ strategy when you enter your room.

3. Language issue.
People with early dementia find problem in speaking basic words and they typically tend to replace them with challenging ones - making it harder for other ones to comprehend. People, for instance, may forget the word 'spoon' and asking in the way "where is that thing with which I eat in some cases?" nevertheless what is typical, is to be not able to find the right word in some cases.

4. Confusion.
Loosing track of dates, passage of time, and the times of the year - and even sometimes, the people tend to be at trouble in comprehending something if it is not instantly going on. Often they even can forget where they are and what are they doing. They can become disoriented with their community too.

5. Misplacement of things.
A person might lose certain normal things at uncommon spots like losing iron in freezer, egg in the draw and so on nevertheless losing of type in wallets temporarily is typical.

6. Poor Judgment.
The victim might dress wrongly in summer season, wearing some warm layers and contrary in winter season.

7. Change in character.
The remarkable change in character of the people in early dementia is seen; puzzled, suspicious, afraid and psychologically depending on other relatives.

8. Losing effort.
The individual with the early Alzheimer illness might become passive in front of television, sitting for hours, and sleeping more than typical duration.

9. Issues with abstract thinking.
The people at early phases have reported to find problem in handling complicated psychological jobs; forgetting numbers series and their use and so on,

10. State of mind swings.
In addition to changes in character of the early phase victim, the unexpected state of mind swings are also reported - from ultra calm to instant ferociousness, from tears to anger and so on, and with no obvious reason.

Discovering, Identifying, and Dealing with Alzheimer s.

Alzheimer's illness is tough to identify. Still today, the only certain technique of Alzheimer's medical diagnosis is through brain biopsies made after the client's death. While this is a particular technique, it is totally backward-looking, like an autopsy. What is needed are positive tests and markers ...
With living clients, the accepted working approach for Alzheimer's medical diagnosis by a procedure of removal. They methodically test for and remove each of the a lot of aspects that could perhaps be accountable for the noticeable, behavior-related signs. Once all of these possibilities are gotten rid of, then Alzheimer's is the only staying possibility, and a medical diagnosis can be made.
Scientists have been hard at work developing approaches and markers for early and certain detection of the starter days of the Alzheimer's procedure of neural degeneration. The objective was to find "markers", be they biochemical, hereditary or physical, with high connection to the start and development of the illness.
The objective is to be able to "see it coming" and gauge its development, so that different brand-new treatments can be begun early. And so their results on the illness in the client can be gauged to evaluate effectiveness, to try different does and after that gauge the actual results.
There is necessary development being made in the location of Alzheimer's medical diagnosis. Hereditary indications have been found, biomarkers are being developed and brain scan innovation is continuously enhancing.
Hereditary. A group at the Translational Genomics Research Study Institute in Phoenix, Arizona, has found a gene called GAB2. If you have a harmed variation of it you are at far higher danger

of ultimately developing Alzheimer's. They are now working to develop a fast and easy test to find the broken gene.

Recognition of the presence of the gene would recognize people who are at danger for the illness later in their lives. It might ultimately help us to detect Alzheimer's illness even right before it begins.

Biomarkers. Nanogen, Inc., a San Diego, CA-based sophisticated innovation business, works to supply scientists, clinicians and doctors with enhanced approaches and tools to forecast, identify, and eventually help deal with illness.

In early 2007 they revealed having actually gotten 2 patents that connect to the recognition of protein biomarkers for Alzheimer's illness. To get a patent they would have needed to show something that is brand-new, distinct and that works.

Brain scan tests, just like an electronic tomography (CT) scan, (the most commonly used), magnetic resonance imaging (MRI) scan, or positron emission tomography (FAMILY PET), in addition to Single Photon Emission CT (SPECT) are now being used. These non-intrusive techniques let doctors have an image of the living brain itself.

These scanning innovations allow healthcare experts to see irregularities within the brain. While they are of great aid in Alzheimer's medical diagnosis, they still have a hard time to get and present great, clear images and info. Nevertheless these are continuously being enhanced. Still, the present level and strength of the search, and the noticeable development that is being made, are motivating indications. Ideally we will quickly have far better approaches for early Alzheimer's medical diagnosis and treatment.

Tension Hormonal agents

Our bodies are hard-wired by nature to respond to tension in a way that was initially meant to secure us against viewed dangers from predators and assailants. The "fight-or-flight" reaction is our natural alarm, and a typical mental and physical response to tension. Tons of the needs of life just like work, traffic, monetary commitments, looking after kids and aging mother and father can trigger your time clock to keep ticking. That increased levels of tension hormonal agents can trigger serious illness in the long run.

When you experience viewed hazards just like a big pet dog barking at you throughout an early morning walk, your hypothalamus triggers an alarm in your body. Through a mix of nerve and hormone signals, this system triggers your adrenal glands, situated on top your kidneys, to launch a rise of hormonal agents, consisting of adrenaline and cortisol. Adrenaline increases your heart rate, raises your high blood pressure and enhances energy supplies. Cortisol, the main tension hormonal agent, increases sugar, or glucose, into the blood stream and boosts your brain's usage of glucose and increases the schedule of compounds that fix tissues. Cortisol also curbs functions that would be inessential or harmful in a fight-or-flight circumstances. It changes body immune system reactions and reduces the digestion system, the procreative system and development procedure.

Generally, after the viewed danger is lessened, the release of tension hormonal agents stops and your body go back to its regular state. This intricate natural alarm also communicates with areas of your brain that control state of mind, inspiration and worry. Extended periods of being stressed out and too much exposure to cortisol and other tension hormonal agents can impact practically all of your body's procedures. This puts you at increased threat of many illness, consisting of:

Heart problem
Sleep Disorders
Gastrointestinal Issues
Anxiety
Weight problems
Memory Disability
Skin problem, Such as Eczema

Scientists at UC Irvine have found that tension hormonal agents also appear to quickly worsen the development of brain sores which are the trademarks of Alzheimer's illness. The findings suggest that handling tension and decreasing certain medications recommended for the senior could decrease the development of the ravaging illness. Frank LaFerla, professor of neurobiology and conduct, and a group of UCI scientists found that when young animals were injected for just 7 days with dexamethasone, a glucocorticoid comparable to the body's tension hormonal agents, the levels of the protein beta-amyloid in the brain increased by 60%. When beta-amyloid production boosts and these protein pieces aggregate, they form plaques, among the 2 trademark brain sores of Alzheimer's illness.

Researchers also found that the levels of another protein Tau also increased. Tau build-up ultimately results in the development of tangles, the other signature sore of Alzheimer's. The findings for this research study appeared in the Journal of Neuroscience. The increased build-up of beta-amyloid and Tau appears to work in a "feedback loop" to accelerate the development of Alzheimer's. The scientists found that the higher levels of beta-amyloid and Tau caused a boost in the levels of the tension hormonal agents, which would return to the brain and accelerate the development of more plaques and tangles. According to the scientists, these findings have extensive ramifications for how to deal with the senior who struggle with Alzheimer's.

"This research study suggests that not only is tension management an important part of dealing with Alzheimer's illness, but that doctors should pay attention to the pharmaceutical items they recommend for their senior clients," said Kim Green, a postdoctoral scientist in Neurobiology and Conduct. "Some medications recommended for the senior people who reside in Assisted Living or Assisted living home environments for numerous conditions consist of glucocorticoids. These drugs might be resulting in sped up cognitive decrease in clients in the early phases of Alzheimer's illness." Alzheimer's illness is a progressive neurodegenerative condition that impacts almost 5 million grownups in the United States. If no reliable treatments are developed, it is approximated that 13 million Americans will be affected with the illness by 2050. Dementia Care is readily available in Assisted Living Facilities Los Angeles along with other significant cities right across the country. Dementia Care is particularly for senior citizens experiencing Alzheimer's illness and other kinds of Dementia.

Alzheimer illness is a neurodegenerative condition which shows progressive dementia and it is the 4th most typical cause of death. There are clear pathological trademarks of the illness, generally in the form of plaques and tangles. Plaques are irregular clusters and pieces of protein, which develop between afferent neuron. Passing away afferent neuron consist of tangles, which are comprised of another protein. These plaques and tangles may be the reason for cell death and tissue loss in the Alzheimer's brain.

Our brain has 3 huge parts: the cerebrum, the cerebellum and the brain stem. The cerebrum is the significant content of our skull. Its primary function is in the parts of recalling, issue solving, thinking, sensation and managing our movement. The cerebellum situated at the back of our head, under the cerebrum and it manages our coordination and balance. The brain stem lies below the cerebrum in front of the cerebellum. It links the brain to the spine and manages functions which are automated, just like breathing, food digestion, heart rate and high blood pressure.

The brain is nurtured by networks of capillary consisted of arteries, veins and blood vessels. The arteries carry blood to sustain our brain with each heart beat.

The distinct external layer of our brain is called the cortex, which is rather plainly mapped according to particular functions. Amongst the significant functions we can see our sight, noise and odor, ideas, issue solving, memory saving and recovering and managing certain motions.

Our brain is split into 2 hemispheres; the left half manages the right body's side and the right half manages the left side. The speech-language location is on the left side in many people. The brain consists of over 100 billion nerve cells or afferent neuron, which branches and produces connections at more than 100 trillion connection points. Brain signals are taking a trip through the network of nerve cells including our memories, ideas, and emotions. Afferent neuron are linked to one another at synapses. A burst of chemicals called neurotransmitters are released at the synapses when activated by the proper electrical charge and so the 'message' is brought to other cells.

Alzheimer's illness is accountable for the damages of those nerve cells and to the interruption of the activity of the neurotransmitters. We also know that Alzheimer's illness causes afferent neuron death and tissue loss throughout the brain. Gradually, the brain diminishes significantly, impacting almost all its functions. Shrinking is specifically serious in the hippocampus, which is a region of the cortex that plays a major role in development of brand-new memories.

Early signs are in the location of learning and memory, thinking and planning, which might disrupt work or social life. At this phase people might get baffled and have issues expressing themselves, organizing and managing cash.

As Alzheimer's advances, people might experience changes in character and conduct and have trouble acknowledging loved ones. People with Alzheimer might live approximately 8 years. In certain cases it perhaps more depends upon other health conditions and other elements like genes.

What triggers Alzheimer?

It is presumed that the cause is a complicated series of events consisting of hereditary, ecological and way of life elements. We do not comprehend the precise cause or the contributions of those aspects and it differs from case to case.

What diagnostic tools are readily available?
Till today, there are no efficient treatments to treat, to stop or to decrease the development of Alzheimer illness. At the exact same time there are a lot of diagnostic tools to recognize the illness, just like non-invasive imaging methods to examine the elements of neuro-anatomy, chemistry, physiology, and pathology of the illness and its evolutionary status.
Among the well-known evaluations is using Magnetic Resonance Imaging (MRI), generally since it makes it possible for the visualization of the brain structures in 3 measurements. Calculated Tomography (CT) is another visualization tool used for the medical diagnosis and assessment of dementia, specifically for cases at early phases. The Positron Emission Tomography (ANIMAL) scan programs brain activity in real-time related to functions just like: reading, hearing, thinking and saying words. High activity parts are marked with red and they reduce in colors as activity level reduced. ANIMAL scan is also used to identify changes in local brain metabolic process. This metabolic over activity is shown as "red-hot-spots" on FAMILY PET images, making it possible for physicians to validate the status of thought cancer location and examine whether they have spread out. Just recently, brand-new gadgets integrating multi-modalities are being developed just like MRI/PET. This is a hybrid imaging innovation that makes use of MRI soft tissue morphological abilities with FAMILY PET practical imaging, which works for cancer detection.

Dealing with Alzheimer's

Handling this illness can be extensive as there is so much that needs to be thought about. The illness itself is in phases and can take 3 months to twenty years to advance; each of these phases will add to daily activities by way of general state of mind, general conduct and thinking. Handling these phases of Alzheimer's can be extremely discouraging undoubtedly, especially if you are the person enduring the suffering.
Throughout the early phases of Alzheimer's there are people who will have the ability to cope well with the illness but as time advances, the later phases might prove all way too much as the intensity of the condition takes its toll and victims are in some cases unable to do anything for themselves and become bed-ridden.
Seeing this happen to a liked one can be amazingly attempting; an experience that one would not really want enforced upon any other person as feelings might run really high and the involved tension might be extraordinary. Nevertheless, if the condition of Alzheimer's Illness has been detected then it is necessary that the right care treatments be followed so as to make sure the client is cared for effectively.
How will you cope? Will you have the ability to cope? All of these questions will really need to be replied to handle the circumstances. You should be prepared and will really need all the info and help you can get to make it through this.

Alzheimer's Caregivers

If you assess your choices you might find that some of the care choices readily available to you consist of at home care, nursing houses, or maybe adult daycare. Other victims might really need more regular guidance, full-time care in the home, or care in a domestic or retirement home. Nursing Residences are over-burdened with dementia victims, specifically those with Alzheimer's illness.

All of these care choices will really need to be pondered when thinking about the best medical care for the Alzheimer's patient. As the illness advances they will really need help more than ever in the past so it is sensible that a structured care strategy be taken into spot.

Security Tips

If you're a caretaker for somebody who has Alzheimer Illness there are some things that you'll want to do to make the home safe for them to life in. Among the objectives of a caretaker is to keep your member of the family, or client, home as long as you can. There are some things that you can do to make the home as safe as possible:

Enhance the lighting in the home. This consists of corridors, staircases, and restrooms. Try to have the exact same level of lighting throughout since changes in light levels can be puzzling for some clients.

Put carpets that are a very different color than the floor or carpets in front of stairs and doors so that the client has a simpler time determining where they are.

Always ensure the client takes their medication while you are watching. You want to make certain that they are taking it and not really missing a dosage.

Block any regions that can be a risk to the client. You can use kid security locks and locks to make tons of regions unattainable, just like knife drawers in the cooking area.

Make certain that the food in the fridge is fresh and not spoiled. People with Alzheimer Illness will typically eat whatever they find despite the taste or condition of the food.

Limitation using some devices in the home, just like the oven/stove, toasters, and knives.

Search for home appliances that come with an automated shut-off gadget. This can stop fires and burns.

Have a list of contact number published at every phone. This consists of telephone number for the cops, fire, physician, toxin control, and relatives.

Check to make certain that smoke detector are working properly.

Keep fire extinguishers throughout the home.

Register with the Safe Return Program. This program helps those people who have Alzheimer Illness make it home securely if they stray and get lost.

Looking after anybody who has Alzheimer Illness needs guidance that is often consistent. This means that you really need to make things as simple on yourself as you can so that you do not spend way too much time keeping your client from things that can hurt them. When you have a house that has plenty of security functions you know that your client is going to be safe. This enables you to concentrate on other elements of home care like looking after your client's feelings and making certain that they still do some of the activities that they delight in doing.

Treatments

Alzheimer's illness is a brain condition in which the brain cells included with memory, judgment, intelligence and conduct go through progressive wear and tear. This significantly impacts one's work, social life and even everyday activities. It can be frightening for the Alzheimer clients and for their instant family or support group to watch the psychological decrease and behavioral changes. Alzheimer illness is the most typical form of dementia and represent 50-70% of dementia cases.
According to data, 5.3 million people in the United States are dealing with Alzheimer's. While Alzheimer treatments aren't present, there is fast effort worldwide to find treatments for the illness, postpone its start, or stop it from developing. Presently, there is no recognized medical remedy for Alzheimer's. Treatments intend to decrease Alzheimer signs instead of treat the illness.

1. Use your mind
This saying is so real. Use your mind. People who stay alert and active are less very likely to develop Alzheimer's in the future in life. Feed your brain continuously with knowledge and include yourself in pastimes and work. Research has revealed that when you learn brand-new things continuously it triggers nerve cells (afferent neuron in the brain) to bind together in brand-new methods. Play trivia, resolve crossword puzzles or learn something brand-new, perhaps join an adult education course. These psychologically revitalizing activities work questions to stop and even decrease illness development.

2. Anti-oxidants
Vitamin A, E and C are effective anti-oxidants actually believed to play a favorable role on brain nerves and memory. Vitamin supplements in addition to food sources of vitamin A, C, E are highly helpful for brain health. Some vitamin A foods are

3. Omega 3 fats
Fish and flaxseeds are called as brain foods as they are wealthy in omega 3 fats. They promote healthy brain functions.

4. Herb

Gingko biloba leaf extract might play a favorable role in treatment of Alzheimer illness, though its role needs more research. Always seek advice from a natural remedy therapist and even your regional specialist right before beginning organic therapy treatment for Alzheimer clients.

5. Great Support Group
It is discouraging to watch a buddy or relative develop Alzheimer. The members of the family typically enter rejection. The caretaker needs to have a ton of perseverance and handle these clients with love, care and understanding.

In the starting phases of Alzheimer's the patients eating practices are typically not impacted and are the exact same as right before they had the illness. Nevertheless, in the later phases this can become a problem and it is necessary that they be kept an eye on to make sure that they are getting the appropriate nutrition. In this I guide on Alzheimer's illness, you will learn some of the standard fundamentals when it pertains to keeping great nutrition for a person who has Alzheimer's.

Alzheimer's Nutrition Fundamentals
As the illness of Alzheimer's advances, it ends up being harder for a specific to preserve the correct eating routines as they tend to forget to eat and have more trouble when doing so. It is necessary that a range of foods consisting of vegetables and fruits are given and that cholesterol and hydrogenated fats are restricted.
It might benefit you to try some littler meals a day in which you can integrate finger foods instead of the standard 3 meals a day as these might be simpler for them to manage.
Nutritional shakes are also a great choice when it concerns providing the extra nutrients they might be not having if they are having problem eating.

The Value of Tracking Hydration
As Alzheimer illness advances, eating along with drinking ends up being harder and it is vital that they get enough fluids as this will stop irregularity and dehydration. The minimum suggestion for fluids is at least 6 to 8 glasses a day.
At mealtimes guarantee that there is always a drink readily available and restrict the table setting to only the required utensils, main course, and drink glass so that there is absolutely nothing else to sidetrack them. It might also be useful to use a drink container with a cover so that they can keep this with them at all times particularly if they tend to roam. You can also try and motivate them by treating them to frozen beverages just like a shakes or an ice cream soda.

Looking After Alzheimer's Clients

If somebody in your family has just been detected with Alzheimer's illness, the news can be distressing and frightening for everybody. You'll be fretted about the changes that you're going to be seeing this person go through along with what the future holds for you as a family. You have already dealt with the very first difficulty: getting the right medical diagnosis. If you're going to be the main caretaker of the relative who has been identified there are some things that you'll really need to know so that you can make life simpler for everybody.

Make certain that you learn as much as you can about Alzheimer's illness and about being a caretaker. You'll want to learn how the illness will impact the other person, what changes will happen, and how you'll have the ability to supply the assistance that is needed so that the person keeps as much of their self-respect and self-reliance as they can. You want to maintain as much of the lifestyle as possible so that everybody included feels a lot like they are still in control and handling alright. The info that you find out about Alzheimer's illness should be shown those people closest to the client, like relatives, good friends, and colleagues. Contact the Alzheimer's Society to find out more since they have a lot of resources that are there for your advantage.

It's crucial that you comprehend that Alzheimer's illness will have a substantial influence on the person who has been identified and their capability to operate. This is an illness that advances over a specific amount of time.

The everyday functions of the person will be considerably impacted depending upon what phase of the illness they are at. You really need to discover the everyday issues that you can expect to deal with as a caretaker. This info will give you a much better grasp of the sensible abilities of the client. Spend some time to ask how you can help them to keep their self-reliance and some feeling of control. Maybe the most essential thing that you really need to learn is how to be client and understanding.

Constantly keep the client in sight. This means that no matter how the illness impacts that client that you always remember that they are a specific with ideas and emotions. Deal with the Alzheimer's client with self-respect and respect at all times no matter how challenging things become for the both of you. A lot of the person's capabilities will be lost but they will still have emotions and feelings that really need to be appreciated.

Medical Treatments

There are certain drugs that can deal with the signs and give victims of Alzheimer's illness a much better lifestyle.

The Options Available for Alzheimer's Drug Treatment:
Whether you yourself are an Alzheimer's illness patient or you are taking care of somebody who is handling the illness, it is best to know whatever you can about the different drugs on the marketplace right before you selecting one to try.

Among the rarely used Alzheimer's drug treatments readily available is Cognex. This is used moderately to fight the results of Alzheimer's because of the lots of negative effects it can result in, for this reason it not being that commonly applauded.

A more typically used Alzheimer's drug treatment is called Exelon, which is a substance abuse to help the early signs of Alzheimer's illness. It helps by slowing the deterioration of psychological expertise, hence helping the victim in their daily life. The loss of control with everyday jobs like dressing, eating and general motor functions are a horrible thing for victim's of the illness, and hence this specific Alzheimer's drug treatment is an advantage for them.

It has already shown itself to be reliable for countless Alzheimer's patients all over the world, and is frequently recommended by Physicians for tons of cases. Physicians typically recommend a dose of 1.5 mg to be taken two times daily, which can be increased every 2 weeks depending upon the requirements of the person.

As the illness advances, the Alzheimer's patient will become more usually depending on outdoors assistance. This might lead to the patient entering into an Alzheimer's treatment centre. Experts at these spots are readily available all the time so as to look after patients, in addition to having the ability to offer any medical support that is needed.

As each Alzheimer's illness victim is a specific in their own right, the sort of Alzheimer drug treatment they really need will differ according to their physician's recommendations. It might still spend some time to select which is the best Alzheimer drug treatment for any given patient, to decrease the adverse effects that are fundamental in these kinds of compounds. Another kind of medication is Namenda, it manages the glutamate that helps the brain to react better to memory and learning. This sort of medication is said to be extremely reliable. In addition to the above pointed out medication, clients were given sleeping tablets to keep away from sleeping disorders. There is also anti-anxiety medication that can deal with behavioral disruption. Finally anti-psychotic medication is used for fear.

Naturally, medical professionals still really believe with non-drug interference. And friends and families can play a vital part of it. If somebody near to you is experiencing Alzheimer's illness, the best medication to administer is love. Their brains might be impacted by the illness, but never ever will his body and soul. Till there is still time, show them you care.

Alzheimer's illness is a progressive degenerative brain illness. Steady amnesia, poor cognitive abilities, dementia and character issues are the primary signs connected with Alzheimer's illness. Though there is not a total treatment for Alzheimer's, Ayurveda has the knowledge to deal with an Alzheimer's client.

Ayurvedic treatment for Alzheimer's illness is very much on its developmental phase. Ayurveda researchers in India, United States and Germany watch of a reliable remedy for Alzheimer's illness using Ayurvedic herbs like Brahmi.

According to Ayurveda, all the illnesses are triggered because of imbalances in body. Tridosha idea is the basis of Ayurvedic knowledge. The food, the day-to-day actions, the idea and other things should be in tune with tridoshas.

Alzheimer's illness is because of imbalance of vata, which prevails in aging. According to Ayurvedic concepts, vata in the tissues of nerve system, particularly brain gets imbalanced. This straight causes issues like lower levels of co-ordination, clear thinking, absence of inhibitions and mentally handicapped words and actions.

Mano vaha srotas or the mind-channel that brings ideas is impacted as a result of vitiation of vata. This is the reason for misconceptions and psychological disruptions.

Once the causes are recognized it is simple to recommend the remedies. In case of Alzheimer's, Ayurveda too offers some help in assisting an individual deal with Alzheimer's.

According to Ayurveda, the stress and tension an individual experience throughout his/her life cause disruptions to vata, the build-up of which triggers extreme anxious issues. Pressure at work, pressure experienced while changing spots, consistent separation from close members of the family, etc. all amount to the psychological conditions.

In India to the big family system of living is quick diminishing. People move into a little family. In the not-so older times, say right before 1980s, Indian families were big with a ton of members of the family. There is assistance for the relatives all the time from other members. This system has consistent strengthening power on individual members and they delight in healthy minds.

1. Vata imbalances are very common in aging. Ayurveda Alzheimer's treatment generally targets at bring back vata balance.
Ayurvedic treatment for Alzheimer's starts with choice of a vata well balanced diet plan. Ashwagandha (Withania somnifera) powder with milk, ghee or skimmed milk according to the digestion capability of the person is the very first re-arrangement in everyday diet plan. This relieves and empowers vata.

2. Daily oil massage right before bath is another vital part of Alzheimer's treatment in Ayurveda. The person at his/her aging need to get enough nutrients. There are specific rice preparations advantageous for individuals who experience the start of or innovative phase of Alzheimer's illness.
Ayurvedic cleaning procedures like panchakarma aren't shown for aged people. Other moderate cleaning strategies like fumigation and enema are directed to cleanse body tissues.

Nervine tonics like brahmi, aswagandha and so on are very important herbs for Alzheimer's treatment.

How to Assistance Really loved Ones

Alzheimer's type dementia is just one of the most incapacitating psychological illnesses. It robs an individual of his/her character and his/her real identity.

Phases of Alzheimer's and Caregiving Assistance
From the really starting phases of Alzheimer's, an individual gradually loses his/her capability to perform standard functions like holding a fork or getting dressed and after that gradually other things like memories disappear. But as a result of a ton of public awareness and good example, more caretakers feel more comfortable looking for resources and assistance so that they have the ability to support and comfort their really loved ones.

Kinds Of Caregiving Activities
In addition to recognizing crucial resources just like medical, support/social services, and governmental programs, caretakers can provide their assistance in other more creative and individual outlets. Kinds of assistance caretakers can provide consist of:

Playing a moms and dad's preferred music or outlining a considerable memory.
Using different types of amusing humor with Alzheimer's clients to help reconnect them to that satisfying experience or activate off a psychological response.

Humor and Alzheimer's.
Since Ronald Regan was detected with Alzheimer's illness, people ended up being more familiar with the significance of looking for resources to get aid while taking care of somebody with Alzheimer's. Humor can usually play a huge role in care.
While people were at first entertained that a previous United States president wanted to play "horsie" with his medical attendants, caretakers seriously thought about humor as treatment for their really loved ones along with for their own tensions. Individuals have signed up with laughter clubs for Alzheimer's to feel more comfortable with their own inhibitions about handling this hard illness.

Alzheimer's Association Supplies More Assistance.
So long as there is no Alzheimer's treatment, caretakers really need to find a way to launch the tension of caregiving. Take a look at the Alzheimer's Association local associations near you. Usually what happens when caretakers share their stories, they learn much from other ones about other methods to help reinforce their really loved ones' memories. It is clear that by offering stimulating and nurturing activities for an Alzheimer's client, one can actually see the love and build a connection, which is as important and vital as the really loved one advances from one phase to another.

The preliminary difficulty for a caretaker is coming to terms understanding that Alzheimer's is a gradually deteriorating illness. Nevertheless, there are a lot of caregiving activities and support system for handling Alzheimer's all around the world.

Treatment Alternatives in a Nutshell

While Alzheimer's illness is not a condition that might be treated at this moment in time, there are tons of treatment choices readily available for those that are identified with this serious brain condition. The objectives of these treatments are to enhance the day-to-day performance of the person that experiences the illness and to enhance the quality level of their life.
In some circumstances, the Alzheimer's treatment choices will actually slow the general development of Alzheimer's. A lot of clients and their family members decide to participate in treatment so as to manage the condition as it advances into the late phases.

Medications
Among the most typical Alzheimer's treatment alternatives is medication. There are various kinds of medications that might be used to decrease the most typical signs of the condition. These treatments work to slow the problem of amnesia, they help vary the state of mind, and even help in the location of enhancing sleep and energy levels for the client. The most typical medications used for this brain illness consist of, but are not minimal, to the following:

Anti-oxidants
Antipsychotics
Sleeping Prescriptions
Cholinesterase Inhibitors
Neuroleptics
Antidepressants
Anxiolytics
Memantine

Education and Assistance
Many individuals do rule out education and assistance when it concerns Alzheimer's treatment choices, but these are actually thought about to be highly reliable treatments. It is very important for both clients and their really loved ones to get an efficient grasp of the illness, in addition to how the illness advances.

Influence on People's Lives

The very first phase of Alzheimer's presents definitely no signs at all and that is why it can never ever be caught. It permits the person to work completely generally and clients who have this will experience no amnesia or any issues. That means that this will not be identified by any healthcare specialists if taken at this phase since it is never emerging in any form. Chances are people will not even go and look for a healthcare expert at all since they will experience no disabilities in phase one. That is why it is great to look for care if you have a relative who has Alzheimer's, especially a moms and dad or grandparent, so you know that it is something to be knowledgeable about.

Phase 2 deals moderate signs like minor amnesia about names, spots and where they put things. The brain might begin to be impacted by the illness in little methods and the client will not keep in mind things that used to be quite clear to them. Nevertheless, despite the fact that some signs start to show, that doesn't mean that this will help it be detected, as lots of people associate the indications that appear in phase 2 as typical indications of aging and getting on in the years.

In phase 3, likewise, there is moderate cognitive decrease, too, but finally the indications revealed suffice to perhaps protect a medical diagnosis of the illness. For example, clients will have a tough time recalling the names of friend or family and not have the ability to keep in mind names of anybody knew they experience. This will produce some efficiency issues at work or in social elements as they will not always remember what to do or how to do it. At this phase, if this is truly uncommon conduct for the person, they can go and get it had a look at and perhaps even detected.

In phase 4, this is when Alzheimer's is normally identified as people cannot keep in mind events, celebrations and even the existing events around them. They are not able to do psychological mathematics and they can no longer do jobs that need a ton of thinking or planning, just like paying expenses or working on hosting a celebration. Individuals forget their own individual history and typically get depressed and melancholy.

Steps 5 and 6 only become worse as people can no longer keep in mind existing specifics about their life and normally get puzzled about the time, the spot, the date, and their environments. As it becomes worse, they will be not able to acknowledge the people around them or perhaps know who they are themselves. They will really need aid getting dressed and will not have the ability to perform normal activities without support.

www.ingramcontent.com/pod-product-compliance
Lightning Source LLC
Chambersburg PA
CBHW081625250726
48657CB00009B/2734